STOP
ADHD, ADD, ODD
Hyperactivity

A Drugless Family Guide To Optimal Health

Robert DeMaria, D.C., D.A.B.C.O.
Director - Drugless Healthcare Solutions™

Stop ADHD, ADD, ODD Hyperactivity
by Robert DeMaria, D.C.

Published by:
Drugless Healthcare Solutions
306 Hamilton Circle
Elyria, OH 44035

Phone: **(440) 323-3841**
Fax:: **(440) 322-2502**
E-Mail: **DrB4Health@aol.com**
Website: **www.DrBob4Health.com**

616.858
D372s

Library of Congress Control Number: 2003091240
ISBN: 0-9728907-0-X

Printed in the United States of America
0 9 8 7 6 5 4 3 2 1

DISCLAIMER
This information is provided with the understanding that the author is not liable for the misconception or misuse of information included. Every effort has been made to make this material as complete and accurate as possible. The author of this material shall have neither liability nor responsibility to any person or entity with respect to any loss, damage or injury caused or alleged to be caused directly or indirectly by the information contained in this manuscript. The information presented herein is not intended to be a substitute for medical counseling.

Page and cover design by One-On-One Book Production

About Dr. DeMaria

Dr. DeMaria has been extremely motivated over the last several years to orient his practice to helping those children who are becoming the pitiful products of the greed, ignorance, apathy and/or total lack of misunderstanding by the medical community, pharmaceutical companies, food manufacturers and parents who are too busy or in a total state of despair about what to do for their children. Dr. DeMaria has been trained and tested in the utilization of nutritional and natural products. He has focused his attention on learning and seeking simple answers to tough questions. Patients of all ages—some with very bizarre histories and persistent conditions—continue to come to his office. These patients are treated with simple measures that, for whatever reason, medicine has ignored.

Beside a chiropractic degree, Dr. DeMaria has a bachelor's degree in human biology, diplomat status in chiropractic orthopedics and a Fellowship in applied Spinal Biomechanical Engineering. He has taught in the legal, insurance, business and health care fields throughout the United States and in Europe. He has been an instructor at Oberlin College. For over twenty-five years, Dr. DeMaria has treated thousands of patients using natural therapeutics. He has been trained to think independently where Western medicine so often limits health care providers into prescribing what the pharmaceutical companies are marketing at the time. He considers it a blessing to be an independent, self-employed health care provider who doesn't worry about pharmaceutical/laboratory kick-backs and hospital jurisdiction. His ability to treat has not been hampered because of this and he continues to attract patients who need help.

When new patients present in his office, he never doubts that he can help that individual. He retraces habits from the beginning to find the root cause of problems—which a change of diet, spinal correction or the addition of basic supplements can correct. He treats patients the way God originally intended—naturally, without drugs.

This book is very exciting. It will change your life. Some of the information contained herein will be disturbing to some. But it works. Draw your line in the sand today. Have you had enough?

Peace and Blessings.
Dr. Bob

Acknowledgments

My wife, Deb, who has lived a drugless healthcare lifestyle since the mid-1970's. Her support and companionship is the cornerstone to our practice and family success.

Our two sons, Dominic and Anthony, have graciously accepted their position as "natural" healthcare kids—and now appreciate their choice.

A special thanks to Christine Gentile, my initial editor and researcher, who took a pile of scribble and thoughts and organized the original manuscript.

All the friends and colleagues who read the book and gave me insight.

The participants in our Pilot Program. They are the real troopers who proved our concepts and understanding of the body as a self-healing creation of God that can correct itself, if given the opportunity.

Finally, all the thousands of patients who accept and understand the role of natural drugless care, living in a society programmed for instant drug cures. I congratulate you!

Thank all of you in advance for sharing the natural drugless care philosophy. It is a principle that will prevail.

RFD

Contents

Foreword to
Stop ADHD, ADD, ODD Hyperactivity
by
Ann Louise Gittleman, Ph.D.

Our kids need help.

Every September I shudder to think how many millions of children go back to school each year for reading, writing and … Ritalin. And while Ritalin may be a "miracle drug" for some, because it has been found to dramatically control (not cure, mind you) hyperactivity symptoms, it is also a Class II controlled substance (think cocaine and methadone) with potential side effects of depression, suppression of growth, stomach aches and lack of appetite, to just name a few.

But the side effects of this medication don't just stop there. Many years ago, a 1995 Drug Enforcement Administration Bulletin listed a whole litany of Ritalin dangers which included how Ritalin abuse can lead to major psychological dependence and how Ritalin could be cancer-causing.

Something is terribly wrong with this picture! Are America's children suffering from a massive epidemic of Ritalin deficiency?

I think not.

I am convinced that the true underlying causes of the symptoms displayed by the attention deficit disorder (ADD) or attention deficit disorder and hyperactivity (ADHD), child like restlessness, short attention span, difficulty with self control, irritability, insomnia, learning problems, mood swings and impulsivity can be found within the nutritional arena. The lack of the proper fats for brain chemistry, excessive sugars and food sensitivities that create biochemical imbalances, environmental toxins, vitamin deficiencies and improper spinal alignments are all contributing to the growing epidemic of hyperactive children.

Of all of these, the best documented is the correlation between nutritional deficits and behavior. In fact research published from 1994-1997 that appeared in the *American Journal of Clinical Nutrition, Magnesium Research, and Biological Psychiatry* showed that ADHD patients are lacking essential fatty acids and the minerals zinc and magnesium. In 1999, the Center for Science in the Public Interest out of Washington, D.C. compiled a report entitled "Diet, ADHD, and Behavior" which contained nearly 20 placebo controlled studies exploring the detrimental effect of diet on children's behavior.

Throughout my nutrition career spanning two decades, I have been working with hyperactive children and therefore, couldn't be more excited and delighted that Dr. Robert DeMaria has outlined a complete program that I can support 100 percent with my readers and clientele. He has laid out a step-by-step plan complete with healthier food options, supplement recommendations, testimonials, name brands, recipes and resources that should be embraced by every single parent in American today. His program helps to set the stage for healthy eating habits and lifestyle changes that are at the very core of our future health.

Won't you share this book with your pediatrician, school system, friends and family members? Better still contact the nation's most influential ADHD support and advocacy groups like the Attention Deficit Disorder Association, CHADD, and the National Institute for Mental Health. It's high time our traditional medical system and national organizations provided Americans with alternative, drugless approaches to ADD and ADHD.

The bottom line is, as you will soon learn in Dr. DeMaria's practical and compelling book, that there are lots of healthier ways to control behavior without resorting to drugs. This book,

Stop ADHD, ADD, ODD Hyperactivity, provides a nutritional and lifestyle cure that is the key to long-term behavior control and lasting good health

Give this program a good three months and you will see how your child's life — and yours will be transformed.

Ann Louise Gittleman, Ph.D.
Coeur D'Alene, Idaho

INTRODUCTION
Greetings!

First, I want to congratulate you for considering the decision to eliminate Ritalin and other behavioral and psychoneurotic drugs from your and your family's life.

I wrote this book as a guide to make a difference in your family's health. My motivation is for you and your family, and particularly your children, to live life in healthy abundance. I treat in a holistic manner patients who have a variety of health conditions. I do not look at one organ at a time. Unfortunately, most health care providers today focus on their narrowed specialty: simply managing symptoms. Often, they will not deviate from their pre-programmed way of medical thinking. I am a natural health care practitioner and understand your struggle with the medical community.

This book is about health. Let's get honest with each other. I want you to read these pages with an open mind and be ready to make changes. It might not be easy. In fact, you still may want to keep your child on medication to keep him/her under control. However, I plead with you—it's a lot easier to make changes today than in the future when your child could have a major issue or chronic disease condition that could have been prevented.

The following pages have the potential of presenting monumental, life-changing methods, ways and ideas for you and your family's optimal health to go to a new level. You are at the mercy of health care providers, researchers, newspaper articles, magazines, periodicals, etc., telling you exactly what is best or most detrimental to your body.

A natural health care practitioner promoting drugless therapies is often very controversial. We live in a drug-oriented society and, as a nation, take billions of prescriptions a year. The average American consumes in excess of twelve prescriptions per year. Thirty-seven percent (37%) of people older than sixty are currently taking five or more prescriptions a day, and nineteen percent are taking seven or more prescriptions a day. Seventy percent (70%) of all infants in the United States are subjected to their first course of antibiotics during the first two hundred days of their lives. More than five million school children are on behavioral medication. It is estimated that up to more than seventy-five million prescriptions a year have been written for Ritalin alone, in addition to other products used in this very competitive market. Over 160,000 people die every year due to drug prescription misuse. Medical mistakes are now one of the leading causes of death in America. This is not an accusation, but a reality check!

> **The average American consumes in excess of twelve prescriptions per year.**

For me, every day is a reality check. "I live in the trenches," as they say. I have practiced holistic health care for 25 years and have seen what drugs do to the body and the psyche. Medical physicians prescribe drugs because symptoms are managed with medication. The American medical system is big business, a woven tapestry of pharmaceutical companies, insurance companies and private practice.

No one has really addressed the underlying cause of hyperactivity, ADD, ADHD and ODD (Oppositional Defiance Disorder). Trust me. There are a lot of variables. I have read and researched articles, books and history. There is no clear picture painted by any particular authority. Most of the information, with a few exceptions, is speculation.

I am not only a health care practitioner, but also a dad. I have two healthy sons with no cavities, no eyeglasses, no medication, no hyperactivity, no asthma and no Ritalin. If I have two healthy sons, then you can also have healthy children. As a sports team doctor for over 10 years, I've stood on the sidelines, I've spoken to youth groups, high schools, elementary, preschool and kindergarten children. They need to be coached; you need to be coached.

Be aware that the content of this book will create a debate. There will be those who will disagree with everything I present because their research reveals differently. Often, the results of research are directly related to the people funding the project. However, there is one concept or fact I believe that most honest individuals can agree upon. Man-made fat or artificially altered natural fats found in our environment and foods are detrimental to our health. Food manufacturers may not agree with this since their livelihood depends on extending the shelf life of products. Yet I see time and again the damage these products are causing.

Man-made fat or artificially altered natural fats found in our environment and foods are detrimental to our health.

We must make a continual effort to understand and be realistic. We need to change the way we think in order to thrive, not merely survive. If we do not change the behavior of chemically-dependent children and adults, then the pharmaceutical companies will continue to profit from their diminished state of health. Remember, they do not treat the root cause of the problem; they instead try to manage the symptoms and ignore the holistic body.

Ignoring the holistic body and only managing symptoms directs us away from the truth behind hyperactivity, ADD, ADHD and ODD. No one seems to know why abnormal behavior and poor mental focus is an epidemic in America. I treat patients by modifying their diets, improving their nervous system function and teaching patients how their body can heal itself. The benefit from this protocol is most often patients with normal behavior and mental clarity. The old saying "an ounce of prevention is worth a pound of cure" is a standard in my practice.

Stop ADHD, ADD, ODD Hyperactivity will facilitate this "ounce of prevention" and explain why there is an epidemic of emotionally unhealthy kids. All you need to do is follow the simple directions, make appropriate changes and get better. I have proved it for over 25 years. It works. I do it daily in my practice. It is simple, easy and logical. You must start now. Spread the good word—tell your friends.

The information in this book will help you recognize why there is a real problem with behavior today. I will explain to you in very specific detail why emotional and behavioral problems are common. You will find information on food groups and alternative foods. Every explanation is to clarify what you need to do to move to the next level of health.

I have offered delectable HYPE-free recipes that recommend alternative ingredients to the foods you enjoy. You will also find information about the food pyramid, how to read labels and the complexity and impact of the fast food industry.

> **Studies have strongly suggested a correlation between a proper nutritional balance in Omega 3 fats and vitamin and mineral supplementation.**

Studies have strongly suggested a correlation between a proper nutritional balance in Omega 3 fats and vitamin and mineral supplementation. Historically, there have been attempts to eliminate specific colors, dyes, and preservatives. While elimination of these components have mixed success in treating hyperactivity, ADD, ADHD and ODD, they have not been consistently useful because many factors were ignored.

Specifically, I explore several topics that have proved useful, such as:

☑ normalizing fat metmetabolism

☑ modifying consumption of refined sugar and the effect it has on the body

☑ recognizing parasites as a hidden cause

☑ revealing a B-complex deficiency

☑ discuss other popular topics including immunization, lead poisoning, the mother's health and birth order

Stop ADHD, ADD, ODD Hyperactivity will not only facilitate diet transformation but also will teach you to nurture personal relationships. I have researched the changing dynamics of family structure, school systems and doctor/patient relationships. These factors, all very plausible, should be considered with an open mind.

Prior to publishing this information, I began a pilot program in which individuals who were not being treated by me for behavioral challenges could participate. The program is laid out in the following pages. The participants utilized the diet program, supplements and natural care I will suggest to you. All products can be obtained at a health food store or natural health care provider. The pilot program was an overwhelming success and will offer motivation and support for your health transition. I have devoted the last part of the book to vital information given by the participants to make your transition easier.

First read the book through slowly and take notes. Do not attempt to make immediate changes in your life. Your circle of friends may challenge what you are doing. Do

Make slow and deliberate lifestyle modifications.

not let anyone dampen your enthusiasm. I do not want you to throw away food. Make slow and deliberate lifestyle modifications. Come to know and experience the benefit of improving family health. Experience less confusion at home and school and have an overall sense of well being.

What you will read really does work. This program will take patience, communication, cooperation and lifestyle modifications. It will be worth it now and in the future. Your entire family's health will improve because of these simple modifications.

Please, enjoy the book and have fun! Let's bring the families in America back together. This is a paradigm-shifting project. Do not be dictated to by those who manipulate what you consume so they can directly fatten their wallets. It is time to stand up, draw a line in the sand and say, "I've had enough!"

Christopher Columbus did what most people thought was impossible. History tells us that at the time of his journey, the world was thought by most to be flat. However, when Columbus embarked on his voyage there were individuals sailing down the coast of Africa who knew that the world was round. Columbus' challenge was going west without an adequate timepiece and the inability to pinpoint his exact destination and location. To the people of his time, Christopher Columbus accomplished "the impossible."

It would seem that our technological advancement would lead us to believe that we could conquer any environmental or personal dilemma. It continues to amaze me that the answers to health care issues always seem to evade us. This can be quite frustrating, especially for the parents of children who have been diagnosed with hyperactivity, ADD, ADHD, ODD, Tourettes and who, later in life, may face the chronic, degenerative conditions.

The educated individuals who lived in major cities like Rome or Madrid told Christopher Columbus that he would have an unsuccessful voyage. People failed to realize that Columbus was an experienced seaman. Those who told him he was doing the impossible more than likely were never in a boat and/or in a position to instruct an experienced captain. They had never experienced Christopher Columbus' challenges of daily life.

There was a terrible condition that plagued sailors called scurvy, a condition that results in bruising, bleeding gums, pain and misery. We don't think about scurvy much today, but if you were the wife or mother of a sailor between the years 1650 and 1850 you would have been concerned. Fifty percent of the sailors that left England never returned home. The cause of scurvy was lack of Vitamin C. It took over 200 years to accept this information. We don't have 200 years to wait while our children are drugged into chemical dependency and lethargy.

I have seen the improvement of many health care dilemmas and have been blessed with the understanding of the body's physiology. The information presented will help you to understand why you and your child are in a lower state of health.

This book and other natural health care information will be mind-stretching but will launch you into an improved level of personal health. These are common sense answers to tough questions.

1

Understanding How You Work– The Basics

Knowledge is Power
Application of Knowledge is Wisdom

Why do you think so many people are sick? Sadly, in our very busy society, few people have a clue how their body works. With access to huge amounts of information, we know so little. The public has been kept in the dark and held hostage. These pages will be necessary for most to have an understanding of "why." The "why" of what I am saying works. If you do not understand the "why," then you won't do it.

You become what you eat, drink, smoke and breathe. What you do affects you! You are directly responsible for your own health. Americans have been programmed to believe that a doctor administering a "magic" pill can fix an abused body. It does not happen that way. Look around. How many people do you know who are healthy, even if taking medication?

It is to your advantage to read through this chapter slowly to get a grasp on how you function.

The Basics: Understanding What Makes You Go!

The Cells

Your body is made up of small units called cells. You have trillions of cells that construct your body. Cells are constantly being replaced. It is estimated you have a new body every seven years. Cells are like little factories. They have an outer membrane that is made up of fat. This is a key point for you to understand. If you consume poor quality fats your body can be impacted at the very basic cellular level in a negative way.

Cells are constantly being replaced. It is estimated you have a new body every seven years.

Cells have energy centers, oxygen areas, and storage compartments that release byproducts of metabolism or waste. There are many different kinds of cells—some are simple, others more complex. Cells of similar types make up tissues, bones and organs. Organs make up a larger group, or organ system (an example would be the digestive system). The digestive system starts in your mouth (where saliva mixes with food) and is completed at the rectum (where the waste products of metabolism are eliminated by your body).

All the systems of the body are interrelated. Modern health care providers do not treat the body as a holistic system. Instead, many health care practitioners believe in aggressively attacking the symptom while neglecting the cause (or why). Attacking the symptom often causes an alteration of cell function and ultimately a disruption of the entire body. Proper cellular function is essential for healing and maintaining a healthy body.

We know cells make up organs. We have several systems I want to discuss to set my foundation. Let's look at the body like we would a car. Every part of the car is interdependent.

The Stomach

The stomach is normally in an acid state. Acid is needed to break down certain foods. Inadequate acid leads to putrefaction and improper food breakdown. It ferments like smelly garbage. We have been told that indigestion is the result of too much acid in the stomach. This is not necessarily true. Remember, not enough stomach acid results in putrefaction which triggers the production of another acid or inorganic acid. This is the acid that results in indigestion. Continual use of antacids can lead to regular digestive distress and poor health. What stops acid production? Age. The older you get, the less acid and enzymes are released and produced. Why is that? Sugar depletes the resources needed to make acid; the more sweets, the more indigestion.

Without acid, you have incomplete food breakdown. Undigested food particles leave the stomach, continue on through your intestines and leave the large intestine through little holes or perforations. This is called leaky gut syndrome. These food particles are picked up by the blood, circulating through the body resulting in allergies, i.e., runny nose, sinusitis, ear infections, lung congestion, swollen hands and ankles.

The food particles circulating are usually protein. Protein, when not digested properly or when there are small undigested amino acids (protein building blocks) present, can precipitate a reaction. Undigested proteins and protein factors, are looked on as foreign invaders within the body. An endorphin release precipitated by these foods may result in your craving more of these foods which causes continued craving and more endorphin release, a feel good cycle difficult to stop. It has been suggested that your blood type may cause you to react differently to certain foods. Regardless, your body can have reactions because of this phenomenon. While milk is the most common allergy culprit, it can literally be any

While milk is the most common allergy culprit, it can literally be any food. Usually what ever you crave is a part of the problem.

food. Usually whatever you crave is a part of the problem—resulting in more endorphins.

The Pancreas

The pancreas is the organ that makes insulin. The pancreas produces insulin to get glucose (blood sugar) into cells. Without insulin, we have huge blood sugar problems. Glucose is your fuel. The pancreas also secretes enzymes, which act like little cargo ships carrying products to and fro. Enzymes break down fats, proteins and carbohydrates (sugars). This is important: By eating food that is fresh—in a natural, not cooked or over-cooked, processed state—your body does not have to work as hard to break it down. Heat destroys enzymes. The more processed and cooked food you eat, the more stress on the body.

Your pancreas also secretes enzymes to assist food breakdown and digestion of what you eat. Undigested food is a breeding ground for unfriendly bacteria and parasites.

There is a new term called "insulin resistance." It appears that if insulin is not able to transport the blood sugar into cells, more insulin is produced, resulting in an up-and-down blood sugar effect in your body. I believe that the fat around the glucose (your blood sugar) and poor functioning liver may be part of this problem. The significance is that your child may be craving sugar because of this simple (yet complicated) problem.

Remember your pancreas also secretes enzymes to assist food breakdown and digestion of what you eat. Undigested food is a breeding ground for unfriendly bacteria and parasites.

The Intestines

The beginning of the small intestines is the area where the liver, gall bladder and pancreas deposit their very important functional digestive juices. Calcium—a very important mineral—is absorbed in the small intestines. As your food continues its journey through the small intestines, villi, or small finger-like projections, continue to absorb nutrients and complete more steps of the digestive process. Food soon reaches the large intestines. The large intestine is a key organ for your child's and your health. Bacteria live in the intestine and are very active in the build-up and breakdown process of nutrients.

Water consumption is needed to keep the bowels moving. This means a pure water source—not soda, not tea, not coffee, not juice—WATER. Would you wash the outside of your body with soda? The water formula is simple. Take your body weight in pounds and divide by 2. The number is the amount of water in half ounces to be consumed daily. Clean machines work better. It is essential that your child have *regular* elimination.Ideally, your bowels should empty shortly after you eat.

The Adrenal Gland

The adrenal glands are located above the kidneys. They have many important functions. They are key in our approach to hyperactivity because of their influence on mineral absorption. The adrenals make natural cortisone—hormones for sexual function—mineral absorbing chemicals, and the chemicals to give you the quick boost if someone yells, "fire." The adrenal glands are stressed when there is over consumption of stimulating foods like caffeine (found in cola, coffee, and chocolate) and sugar. Signs of mineral deficiencies (especially potassium) and weak adrenals can be: blood pressure droping from a sit to stand position, bright light bothering the eyes and difficulty in swallowing. Mineral depletion is common today. **Minerals are needed to help solve the hyperactivity puzzle.**

> **The adrenals make natural cortisone— hormones for sexual function— mineral absorbing chemicals, and the chemicals to give you the quick boost if someone yells, "fire."**

The Nervous System

Finally, let's address one of the most important systems: the nervous system, which controls the function of the body. Your brain is the master computer. A large cable called the spinal cord leaves the brain. Smaller nerves, called cranial nerves, leave the brain and also affect organs and tissues. There are a variety of nerve fibers and nervous systems. Every part of your body has a connection to the brain, either by a direct link or indirectly through a mass of little connections.

The nervous system is the most important organ system because it is the only unit partially encased in bone. Subluxation, or misalignment of vertebra (spinal bones), alters body communication. The spinal cord is in the vertebra column. The nerves leave the cord at various areas and go to tissues, other organs, and bones. We are literally connected by a huge mass of wires. It has been suggested that if you remove all the flesh from a person, but leave the nerves, you can make out the form of a person. Quite awesome!

A patient gave me a written testimony on her son's dramatic improvement with dietary changes and normalization of nervous system function with spinal correction and dietary care. Her statement said the following:

> *"My son's ADHD/depression/seasonal stress disorder and stomach pains originally brought us into the office. In a little less than one month's time, my son's depression has decreased greatly. In October, when the time changes, his mood swings seem to really increase. We can usually set our calendar to it. This year we have seen no sign of it. He seems to be his usual self, and he is in better spirits. He has struggled since he was four years old. He has been on many medications, including Ritalin, which made him aggressive. Clonidine and Wellbutrin "zombies" him out. He now takes Nortriptoline for the ADHD, but again, nothing seemed to help. We are cautiously optimistic since this will be the first year in the past six or seven years that Jon, and we as a family, will not have to deal with this and look forward to him getting off of the medication for the ADHD."*

You can take pills and potions to improve symptoms and change chemicals in the body, but unless the information from the brain is sent and received by the organs, you will not see total healing or correction.

Many volumes are written on nervous system function. This young man apparently had interruption of signals from his brain to and through tissue in his body. I tell these patients that the power's off, much like a breaker is shut off or a fuse is blown. You can take pills and potions to improve symptoms and change chemicals in the body, but unless the information from the brain is sent and received by the organs, you will not see total healing or correction.

Mary, one of our adult participants, had more energy and less menstrual cramping the first twenty-three days into the program. She was very excited because her psoriasis started to go away. She noticed positive changes two weeks into the program. Her headaches lessened. A side benefit for Mary was her four- and twenty-month old babies' behavior and sleep improved. Mary really felt the Omega 3 fats helped a lot.

Your body is a wonderfully made piece of equipment that naturally compensates for any imbalance. Unfortunately, this natural compensation stresses the body.

The lifestyle decisions you guide your child to make affect the outcome: a healthy or unhealthy future. Positive choices result in optimal health; negative choices result in poorer quality of life.

> Approximately one million cells must be replaced every hour—24 billion cells a day

NOTES:

2

A Ritalin Nation

Since 1995, the media has uncovered much about Ritalin and America's children. Ritalin use has reached a new level within American society. Children as young as four are prescribed the drug, college students crush and snort Ritalin for its rush and middle-aged adults use it to help with concentration.

Maybe you don't realize how widespread Ritalin use affects our schools and our neighborhoods. Read your newspaper, listen to the news, then make your own assessment about America's drugged children. News articles reflect our present state as a **Ritalin Nation**.

The prescribing of Ritalin is big business for pharmaceutical companies, HMOs and those who sell Ritalin on the streets. *USA Today* published one story titled, "Stealing, Dealing and Ritalin." The article highlights how a black market has developed for the sale of Ritalin. It has been reported that students avoid taking their prescribed Ritalin only to sell the drug at a higher price to fellow classmates. Some also admit to stealing Ritalin from an affected sibling and selling it. It has been reported that school principals steal the prescriptions from the students and then sell them on the streets at anywhere from $5 to $20 a pill.

Parents are also using their children to get prescriptions for Ritalin. Adults report that Ritalin gives them a sense of "euphoria, greater energy and productivity, increased sexual appetite, and overall feeling of being a lot smarter."

Ritalin has not only become big business among children and parents but also with the government. Consider this article from the *American Almanac*, written by Michele Steinberg:

> *"On June 22, Pennsylvania State Rep. LeAnna Washington (D.Phila.), testified at an Ad Hoc Dem. Hearings, stating: 'In 1987, Attention Deficit Hyperactivity Disorder (ADHD) was literally voted into existence by the American Psychiatric Association.' Within one year, 500,000 children in the United States were diagnosed with this affliction. In 1990, the lucrative doors were opened to a cash welfare program for low-income parents whose children were diagnosed with ADHD. A family could get more than $450 a month for each child. In 1989, children with ADHD made up 5 percent of the disabled population. In 1995, it rose to 25 percent. In 1991, education grants also funded schools an additional $400 in annual grant money for each child. The same year, the Department of Education recognized it as a handicap and provided children with special services. In 1997, some 4.4 million children were diagnosed with ADHD. In September 1996, $15 billion was being spent annually on the diagnosis, treatment, and study of these so-called disorders."*

Ritalin and similar drugs are prescribed to an estimated five million children and adolescents in the United States. This is why Ritalin production has increased an incredible 700 percent since 1990.

With the rise in "hyperactivity" diagnosis came the rise in prescribing the drug. What is more frightening is that children are being prescribed various combinations of these psycho-active drugs. **They are being used as unmonitored guinea pigs.**

These psychoactive drugs could be a cause of teenage suicide and violence against others. More and more we hear of school shootings and violence within our schools. Many of the child-killers involved in Littleton, Colorado-style incidents were taking mind-altering psychiatric drugs prescribed by doctors. T.J. Solomon, the 15-year old from Conyers, GA, who shot six classmates in May 1999, was taking Ritalin; Eric Harris, age 18, one of the two Columbine killers, was taking the anti-depressant Luvox; Kip Kinkel, the 15-year old from Springfield, Oregon, who killed both his parents and two schoolmates and wounded 20 other students in May 1998, had been taking the anti- depressant Prozac, one of the most widely prescribed drugs today.

Understand that psychoactive drugs inhibit the nerves from sending clear information to the brain. These individuals often cannot rationalize their behavior and may act out violently toward themselves and others. We are faced with a serious problem when more than six million kids under 18 are prescribed Ritalin, Luvox, Prozac, Paxil and other anti-depressant/psychiatric drugs.

A more serious and frightening problem arises when young children are prescribed mind-altering drugs. I have regular conversations with parents who are unhappy with their toddlers being placed on drugs. A common question is, What has happened with patience? Patience is needed for children, especially children under four years of age. Anyone who diagnoses a child ADD, ADHD, Hyperactive, or ODD and places that child on medication should themselves be evaluated. Instead, interventions, dietary changes and holistic health care should be pursued. Bonding and attachment issues between child and mother should be evaluated. However, those individuals who have true neurological imbalances, those children who when given a specific direction do the opposite and/or exhibit behavior of which they are totally unaware, will more than likely have the symptomatology of hyperactivity.

It is not uncommon to see young children consuming french fries, sugar and other hydrogenated fats that will cause imbalances as soon as they cut teeth.

How do children develop this condition? It is not uncommon to see young children consuming french fries, sugar and other hydrogenated fats that will cause imbalances as soon as they cut teeth. While I do not believe that a child under the age of four should be on medication, I do believe that there needs to be an investigation into what that child is eating.

The Three Muskateers

Tom, Dan and Kathy are a part of a blended family. There was a fourth but she opted not to participate in our pilot study. What was interesting about the three is they didn't seem to pay attention or care at the beginning but did the best overall. Dan had purple, spiked hair. Kathy was jibbering constantly and Tom stared and smiled at our introductory seek-and-find meetings. Their mother was maxed out from dealing with four teenagers. One of the comments made was Kathy wanted the noise out of her head. She had been plagued with this forever. She was taking three different medications regularly. Kathy and her brothers consumed dairy and fried food daily. During the program, the family worked together as a team. Tom was able to go off Ritalin. Dan was not on anything yet but scheduled to start—he didn't. Their journal revealed they had days with cravings, and days without cravings, for sugar and fried foods. The cravings disappeared over time. Their emotional-behavior symptoms were gone within three weeks. Kathy's noises in her head left soon into the program. All three went from Fs, Ds and Cs to As during the school year.

Diagnosis and treatment of hyperactivity, ADD, ADHD, ODD is difficult. There is a continuing debate as to when a child should or should not be labeled hyperactive, ADD, ADHD or ODD. Who needs to be involved with the treatment of a child that has had neurological dysfunction? Doctors and schools must communicate with the children and the parents. There needs to be improved follow-up. Teachers, as well as parents, will play a key role in successfully treating ADD. And we all must give special attention to what our kids are eating!

Finally, there is a growing discussion about women who are diagnosed as hyperactive. Signs of hyperactivity are far different in young girls than in boys. Young girls show symptoms like being overachievers, talkative or being a tomboy. As there has been little research on girls and hyperactivity, doctors are now redefining hyperactivity for fcmales. The article "Ritalin: Mom's Little Helper" explains that adult women now use Ritalin for concentration and motivation. This becomes a difficult diagnosis for doctors to make: does the patient really need Ritalin or does she need to simplify her life?

The media will cover Ritalin use and hyperactivity, ADD, ADHD, ODD more and more as the topic becomes more heated. Media has also covered the connection between hyperactivity, ADD, ADHD, ODD and divorce, Ritalin use among college students, and the frightening over-diagnosis and over-prescribing of Ritalin in the United States. This topic will become even more prominent once readers of this book utilize this program. I am not highlighting what I found in the media about Ritalin use to scare you. I want you to know that diet, exercise and maintaining a balanced body will eliminate frightening drugs from your lifestyle. You will make history by participating in this movement to stop the drugging of children in our Ritalin Nation.

...diet, exercise and maintaining a balanced body will eliminate frightening drugs from your lifestyle.

Two Boys Made It Against The Odds

Harry and David were two young boys caught up in a system that could have led to long-term Ritalin use. The boys attended a parochial school. Their mother was a part-time secretary at the school. Her clerical work helped pay their tuition. She came from a Northern Europian background and her husband was from the Mediterranean area. She saw our Pilot Program request form posted at the grade school. Like many people, she never heard or knew anything about natural drugless health care. This was all new to her.

Harry was on Ritalin and David was supposed to go on it. Surprisingly, the boys mother took Harry off his Ritalin the same time they both started our program. Ironically, two weeks into the lifestyle change, a school personnel mentioned to the mother how much better David was doing on Ritalin. The school never knew Harry and David were both doing excellent without medication. The boys were complimented for their much improved school work, concentration, attendance and behavior as their school year ended. David lost weight, his depression left and his concentration increased. Harry had very similar results.

A very common realization by the participants and my patients is the fact that they can control their own destiny with proper choices. They do not have to be dependent on drugs!

USA Today *reported that a recent study on ADHD and substance abuse, found that "Kids treated with stimulants were more likely to try cocaine in high school..."*

~

An article in The Wallstreet Journal *reports that a study by addiction specialists at Harvard University believe that one of the reasons cocaine users get sick so often is that "the drug restricts production of a body protein that triggers immune responses."*

3

Links to Hyperactivity

Hyperactivity – Attention Deficit Syndrome/Attention Deficit Hyperactivity Disorder –

Writing this book gave me an opportunity to reminisce on my childhood. I see my mother calling us in for dinner while I turned the corner riding my "Huffy." We did not have food processors, a microwave, food slicers and dicers. My sandwiches were wrapped in wax paper and carried to school in a brown paper bag.

Food preparation was never quick and certainly never came in the form of a T.V. dinner. Cooking was always an event, bringing the family together to laugh, cry and sometimes drive each other a little crazy. It was not until the early 1960s that fast food made its way to our town. I remember the excitement, the lights and the thrill of eating out. It was a "treat," something we did once or twice a year.

As a baby boomer, I was in grade school during the late 1950s and early 1960s. Large families were the norm and most of my friends were in families where four to eight siblings were common. Thinking back, I can't really remember many kids acting out in a classroom of 33. We just didn't have any students labeled ADD.

Ask any teacher today about classroom behavior and they unanimously report that they have several behaviorally-challenged children in their classroom. This problem is growing every year; the classroom program has become 80 percent discipline and 20 percent learning.

The label of hyperactive has come to encompass a variety of behaviors and emotions. "When I use the term "hyperactivity," stated Dr. Braly, author of *Food Allergy and Nutrition Revolution*, "I mean it to include a broad category of emotional, mental and behavioral problems: constant movement, destructiveness, abusiveness, inability to concentrate or to sit still, moodiness, nervousness, anxiety, fright, migraines, distractibility and stubbornness. These students fall behind in class. They irritate teachers and their peers and can drive their parents to distraction. They're reckless about safety and often try dangerous stunts. They can't sleep, are often bed-wetters and/or wake up with nightmares."

Behavioral problems still remain a big mystery to some. Primary contributing factors for the behavioral and emotional challenges I see today are directly associated with nutrient deficiencies, especially essential fatty acids (EFA). These deficienies result in inflammation, allergies and joint pain. **Hyperactive children—especially those from families with a history of hay fever, hives, asthma, eczema or muscle pain, for example—are either unable to metabolize essential fats properly or are, frankly, EFA deficient.**

Hyperactive children may complain of abnormal thirst. This is related to problems with the intestinal lining and the role of fatty acids in the strengthening of tissue membrane. Small perforations occur in the intestines, water literally leaks out and the individual becomes thirsty. Proper EFA metabolism is needed for healthy cell walls. **A breakdown in fatty acid production will result in many bodily symptoms.**

The role of essential amino acids (protein building blocks), zinc, vitamin B6 and magnesium are important, since low levels inhibit the production of prostaglandins, an end product of EFA synthesis. Many hyperactive children have low levels of these nutrients.

Often hyperactive children are miserable with themselves. At a local dentist's office recently, a young patient was in the waiting area having a conversation with himself. My wife glanced over at him and he soon realized what was occurring. Afterward he was making slight hand motions to himself to tell himself to be quiet. Imagine what was going on in his head. Participants in our program told me of constant thought and activity going on in their minds. These individuals appear to go nonstop 24-7. When these problems are caught early, dietary changes can quickly eliminate symptoms. If left unattended, problems may become compounded, anti-social behavior becomes ingrained and schoolwork is neglected. Even if the problem is diagnosed at a later age, dietary changes work, but can take longer to become effective and often are coupled with social problems. It is not always easy to change the lifestyle habits of people who are accustomed to convenience foods. Thus, one advantage of a diagnosis at age four results in examining diet, supplement needs and spinal adjustment care instead of relying on medication.

It is not always easy to change the lifestyle habits of people who are accustomed to convenience foods.

According to statistics, Ritalin production has increased 700 percent since 1990 and the U.S. uses 90 percent of the world's production of Ritalin. It amazes me the number of children that go from Ritalin to Clonidine, Paxil and Prozac, a very common sequence today. An accepted treatment for hyperactive children today (by non-nutritionally oriented doctors) is a combination of Ritalin therapy and counseling. Ritalin and Adderall (an alternative drug used to treat behavioral-challenged patients) treat only the surface manifestations of hyperactivity and bring only temporary, symptomatic relief. They are also fraught with side effects.

A very startling comment is that it is "easier" to take a pill than to make lifestyle changes. Our current cultural mindset may in fact be a part of the overuse of medication to control behavior. Ritalin is essentially a form of amphetamine, a stimulant of the central nervous system. It makes a normal adult behave hyperactively, but it has the paradoxical affect of calming a hyperactive child, so much so that it may turn him into a dull, unresponsive, semi-aware robot. It's not much of a trade-off. This represents a failure to understand and properly treat the underlying problem with diet and proper care of the nervous system.

What are some of the potential side effects of Ritalin?

☑ Stunted growth

☑ If abruptly discontinued, it can bring on depression and suicidal feelings

☑ May lower the attack threshold of young patients with a prior history of seizures and induce more frequent seizures

☑ Cause adverse reactions in combination with anticoagulant drugs (blood thinning drugs), anti-convulsants and anti-depressants

☑ Commonly causes extreme nervousness and insomnia

Other Reactions Include:

☑ Skin Rashes
☑ High fever
☑ Arthralgia (joint pain)
☑ Dermatitis (skin inflammation)
☑ Internal hemorrhaging
☑ Loss of appetite
☑ Nausea
☑ Dizziness
☑ Palpitations (heart beat alterations)
☑ Headaches
☑ Dyskinesia (impairment of voluntary movement)

☑ Drowsiness
☑ Changes in pulse and blood pressure
☑ Angina
☑ Chest pain
☑ Cardiac arrhythmias
☑ Abdominal pain
☑ Weight loss
☑ Reduction in white blood count
☑ Anemia
☑ Loss of appetite
☑ Hair loss

Other individuals site allergies as a cause of hyperactivity. Improper fat metabolism is the key that starts that sequence resulting in these allergic reactions. In my clinical experience, patients have food sensitivities to the common foods they consume because their intestinal walls have perforations from poor cell membrane function that has resulted from faulty fat metabolism. Our patients in the Pilot Program confirmed this with food allergy testing.

There is one more very interesting point to be made about hyperactive children: hyperactive males outnumber females about three to one. Also consider the fact that males require an essential fatty acid intake about three times higher than that of females to prevent deficiency. This provides an explanation as to why males are more susceptible to hyperactivity. And it indicates that supplementation for males should perhaps be considerably higher than that for females.

> ...hyperactive males outnumber females about three to one...But recent research shows that girls and women exhibit a different form of ADD, often labeled as "ADD without hyperactivity."

But recent research shows that girls and women exhibit a different form of ADD, often labeled as "ADD without hyperactivity." Girls and women exhibit the symptoms of having poor organizational skills, inability to complete a task, shyness, anxiousness, and withdrawal, spacey or even depressed. Following the program outlined in this book will minimize these symptoms.

Dr. Johanna Budwig, an internationally-recognized authority in the physiology and utilization of fats as well as seven-time Nobel Prize nominee, concurs with Dr. Braly, Clinical Nutritionist Ann Louise Gittleman and others, on the role of proper fat metabolism and health. She understands the role of unsaturated fats (flax oil) in children's health and states, "A lack of highly unsaturated fats is particularly noticeable in connection with brain and nerve functioning. An adjustment in diet to one with oil and protein contents high in unsaturated fats brings the best results in children… I recommend that the whole family adjust their food intake so that they use the optimal, natural fats. As for children whose scholastic performance is often below normal—and it's usually the case in families where the *parents don't eat correctly*—the results of an optimal fat intake normally begin to show themselves in school marks being *bettered*."

I want to make a few bold statements. You will improve your family's level of health by following the recommendations in the pages of this book. You will not be dependent on drugs. You will spend less money buying drugs that manage symptoms, and your doctor bills will dramatically drop. (Who will be unhappy with this?) Simple dietary changes can foster enormous improvements. Medication is not the only answer to treating a patient. Proper food consumption provides building blocks for proper fat metabolism. Proper fat metabolism will then result in proper nerve transmission function and, therefore, healthy behavior. You will not suffer "side effects" by making proper food choice. We are deficient in the proper consumption and utilizations of fats and this is affecting our health. It is time to return to what was once normal. If you do not alter your family's abnormal health patterns, you and your child's health will reflect a lower state of optimal living.

> Millions of Americans 12 years and older
> misuse or abuse prescription drugs,
> a problem that can be deadly.

4

Fact #1: Improper Fat Metabolism

The Number One Reason Why Your Child Is in a Hyperactive-Attention Deficit State

This may surprise you: Your body needs fat to function. Your body utilizes fat to make cell membranes, including the covering that protects the nerves. Fat cushions nerves, enabling the electrical signals being sent to reach the destination in a proper, timely and uninterrupted manner. This must occur with the highest quality nutrients available. If there is a breakdown in this process, you will have an unhealthy body which so many accept as normal.

> **Fat cushions nerves, enabling the electrical signals being sent to reach the destination in a proper, timely and uninterrupted manner. This must occur with the highest quality nutrients available.**

One way to understand the reasons for many of today's health challenges, including mental and behavioral disorders, is to look at the foundations of good health and how fat fits into that picture. Changing your attitude toward fat in your and your child's diet may be challenging, especially after being bombarded with the low-fat lifestyle for so many years. But fat isn't all bad, no matter what you've read or heard. More and more health professionals are calling attention to this misconception. John Finnegan, author of *Facts about Food*, states that "the fats and oil story may well be the greatest scandal of ignorance and disinformation and greed in the entire history of food production."

Ann Louise Gittleman, M.S., in her book *Eat Fat, Lose Weight: How the Right Fats Can Make You Thin for Life*, states:

> "There is frightening evidence to suggest that the previous three generations of **Americans have not been eating the right kinds of fatty acids for the development of the brain**. Could this be a reason we have so many children diagnosed with attention deficit hyperactivity disorder (ADHD)? America's children are being diagnosed right and left with ADHD and are being prescribed the drug Ritalin. These kids are not suffering from a Ritalin deficiency. There are studies to suggest that these children are suffering from essential fatty acid (EFA) deficiency because some of the clinical signs of EFA deficiency are restlessness, short attention span, irritability, mood swings, and even panic attacks. When children diagnosed with ADHD start eating the right kinds of fats, many parents notice that their children become calmer and more focused."

Over the last twenty or thirty years it has been suggested that the low-fat diet is key to long-term health. This is not entirely wrong. I am not suggesting that you should eat a huge steak, ice cream and other "saturated" fat foods. *I am trying to ask why, even with this low-fat mania, we continue to have epidemics of obesity and heart problems?* Heart conditions will continue to plague our society and continue as long as we persist in our current eating practices.

The major building blocks of all fats are fatty acids.

Fat is one of many components and nutrients needed for a healthy body. The major building blocks of all fats are fatty acids, and there are many specific fatty acids that the body uses to function optimally. A pair of these acids, called **Essential Fatty Acids (EFA)**, cannot be made by the body. They must be eaten, digested and processed through specific steps to be properly integrated for optimal body function.

Chemistry 101 – This will require *focus*!

There are many classifications and categories of fats. The first EFA is called Linoleic Acid, which is literally an acid. Some of the names for these fats are related to the position of bonds or links. There are other names that refer to the length of the chemical blocks or chain size. Linoleic Acid is a part of the Omega 6 family; the omega position is determined by the placement of the double bond(s). This particular EFA (Linoleic Acid) can be a precursor of other fats but cannot be made by the body. That is why it is called an essential fatty acid. Foods such as sunflower oil are considered precursor foods, so named because they need to be consumed in conjunction with other foods for the body to use those foods effectively. Sunflower oil, for example, will go through steps to become what will eventually be used by the body as an "essential fatty acid." **The steps are important. (see Chart #1, page 35) Having inadequate nutrients can interfere with the processing of precursor foods from the diet, primarily vegetable oils, nuts and certain leafy greens. There is widespread misconception about why certain people cannot process fat and other foods effectively. I have had patients tell me that they were told they were "genetically" incapable of processing fats properly. Yet, with nutritional supplements and dietary modifications, they were seeing improvements within two weeks. My experience suggests that eating demineralized, refined or processed foods inhibits the body's ability to process EFAs.** *This is a key point.* Omega 6 fat can be processed to make other fatty acids and one which can be directly obtained from dietary sources called Arachidonic Acid. The other essential fatty acid, Alpha Linolenic Acid is known as an Omega 3 fat, and results also in the formation of Docosahexaenoic (DHA) and Eicosapentae-noic (EPA) necessary for a healthy nervous system.

Prostaglandin Function

EFAs function as building blocks for membranes of every cell in the body. They also help produce "prostaglandin families," which are necessary for energy metabolism, cardiovascular and immune health. Prostaglandin is a fat-tissue-like hormone and is part of the end metabolism of fats. It is critical for proper health, including emotional and behavioral states. This is one of the reasons that the diet choices, cardiovascular diseases and other major conditions we are plagued with today are inter-related. You will read much more about this later.

Prostaglandins are important for the regulation of inflammation, pain, swelling, blood pressure, heart function, gastrointestinal function and secretions, kidney function and fluid balance, blood clotting and platelet aggregation (stickiness), allergic response, <u>nerve transmission</u>, and <u>steroid production</u> and <u>hormone synthesis</u>. As you can see, **prostaglandins and EFAs are vital to proper body and neurological functioning!**

The process that creates prostaglandin is connected to EFAs and also includes several steps. In humans, the Omega 3 and Omega 6 essential fatty acids are ultimately converted, via metabolic pathways, to three different series of prostaglandins, each serving an important function.

Three prostaglandins will be a part of our discussion. **Prostaglandin #1 and #3 help reduce pain and are viewed as "good."** They also stop blood cells from sticking together, helping to make blood vessels soft and pliable. **Prostaglandin #2 has pain-producing properties and is viewed as "bad." Prostaglandin #2 promotes platelet stickiness, which leads to hardening of the arteries, heart disease, and strokes.**

☑ The term "Omega" designates the location of a chemical bond or link in the fat chain.

☑ Omega 3 fats are used to make prostaglandin #3; Omega 6 fats make prostaglandin's #1 and 2.

☑Prostaglandin #1 and 3 must balance the effects of Prostaglandin #2.

Prostaglandin #1 Primarily sourced from Omega 6 Fats	Prostaglandin #2 Primarily sourced from Omega 6 Fats and directly from the following:	Prostaglandin #3 Primarily sourced from Omega 3 Fats
☑ **Primrose Oil** ☑ **Black currant Oil** ☑ **Borage Oil** ☑ **Safflower Oil** ☑ **Sunflower Oil**	☑ **Dairy** ☑ **Red Meat** ☑ **Mollusks** ☑ **Shellfish**	☑ **Flax Oil** ☑ **Greens** ☑ **Algae** ☑ **Selected nuts** ☑ **Fish–directly sourced from fish**

Improper Fat Metabolism

Why are man-made synthetic and hydrogenated fats a problem?

Having treated thousands of patients, I believe there must be one significant link between current diet trends and the health challenges facing us today. These dietary habits are also linked to hyperactivity, ADD, ADHD, and ODD. The role of EFAs and prostaglandin in the healthy function of the nervous system are key to understanding and treating these problems.

> **The role of hydrogenated fats and the breakdown of proper fat metabolism is a very significant factor in behavioral challenges. Hydrogenated fats—which have permeated every component of our food chain—stop your body from processing the material needed to send vital messages along nerve fibers and in the brain.**

Eating man-made fats, (olean™ and appetize™) or animal fats that are highly saturated does not promote good health. All fats are not bad; you must consume healthy fat (selected plant, animal, fish, and derivative foods) in order to have your body metabolize food properly. A part of the challenge today is that we consume too many hydrogenated fats (also called "trans-fatty acids" or "partially hydrogenated fats"). These are plant oils that have been heated at high temperatures with added hydrogen. **These fats are unhealthy because they prevent the body's proper use of "good" fat (Omega 6 and Omega 3 fats) for EFAs, causing numerous health problems.** If our consumption of these fats continues, our life expectancy will plummet!

The process for hydrogenated fat was developed in 1873. At that time, there was a major movement by the dairy association to keep the new process under control. Prior to World War II, the American public was accustomed to eating butter. Because of World War II, an alternative to butter was developed under the name of "oleo margarine" and marketed to the public. In time, cardiovascular disease became very common in the western world. Research determined that high cholesterol and high fats were contributing factors to the rise in heart disease. We were led to believe that these transfatty acids (**or hydrogenated fats) from vegetables did not increase cholesterol or saturated fats in the body. Man-made fats are, in fact, a factor in depressing HDL cholesterol, the "good kind of fat" and raising the LDL cholesterol, "the bad kind of fat."** Margarine is not a food and is actually a cause of heart and blood vessel disease. Natural health care providers have been stating this belief for many years.

Hydrogenated fats are commonly seen in fast food restaurants in the form of french fries and various other fast foods. Originally, french fries were cooked in lard. The fast food industry was very excited when lard was eliminated because this reduced cost and increased profits. Lard is from animal sources and is more costly than easy-to-produce hydrogenated oils. Lard, as well as hydrogenated oils, is not heart healthy. Salad dressing is also a common source of hydrogenated oils including dressings served at restaurants. Read labels. Take a moment now and look through your cupboards. Most of the commercially prepared foods have hydrogenated fat in them because they have a longer shelf life.

Consumption of precursor foods with oils from corn, safflower and sunflower are needed for the body to function at an optimal level. Black currant and evening primrose oils do not need to be synthesized as do the other precursor oils.

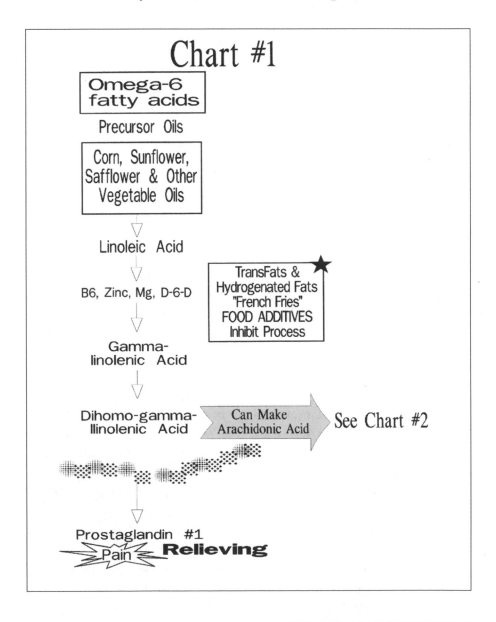

Please note in Chart #1 the large arrow indicating that this fat process can be used to make another essential fatty acid called arachidonic acid. **Arachidonic acid is a pain-producing fat that can be *directly sourced* from meats, organs, shellfish and dairy fats, including milk.** Consuming *too much* of these foods can lead to an imbalance of the very important ratio of Omega 6/prostaglandin #1 and 2 precursors and Omega 3/prostaglandin #3 precursors. This may be a reason dairy products (cottage cheese, commercially-prepared yogurt, ice cream, pizza, etc.) can be a factor in hyperactivity.

As you will note in Chart #1, these precursor oil foods need Vitamin B6, zinc (Zn), magnesium (Mg) and an enzyme called Delta-6-desaturase (D-6-D) to be a part of this process. Your body needs these building blocks (and other nutrient factors) to make a prostaglandin.

To eliminate B6, Zinc or magnesium would be like making concrete without sand. The concrete would fall apart. Processed and devitalized foods rob your body of these substances resulting in poor prostaglandin and fat metabolism in the body. **This is an important consideration as to why people of all ages who consume processed food are in a low state of health and the reason why we have rampant hyperactivity, ADD, ADHD, and ODD in our society today.**

Cells are the basic structures making up all tissues and organs. Proper fat metabolism is necessary to create the proper material to make the cell walls. Your body sends information along the nerve by way of the myelin sheath, which is made of fat. Interfering with this pathway may result in improper nerve function and brain information transmission.

In other words, **what you eat is affecting you**. The increased incidence of emotional and behavioral problems is directly associated with the improper metabolism of fat caused by what you choose to eat. **In my practice, not only do I see behavior affected, but most pain syndromes and other functional conditions (including asthma, fibromyalgia, tendonitis, chronic fatigue, psoriasis, liver congestion, headaches, menstrual pain, constipation, etc.) are directly linked to the condition of this metabolic pathway.** We are experiencing a nose dive in our quality of health because of "man-made convenience foods." We have helped thousands of patients by balancing this mechanism of body function.

> **The half-life of transfatty acids or hydrogenated fats is 51 days.**

The half-life of transfatty acids or hydrogenated fats is 51 days. That is, after 51 days, one-half of the negative effects of this man-made fat have been processed, but the body needs an additional 51 days to complete the process. After these 51 days, there is still a 25 percent residual. Therefore, the ill effects of one bag of fries lasts 102 days! Can you believe it? Scary, but true!

> **It takes over three months (102 days) to minimize the negative effect transfatty acids and hydrogneated fats (as found in french fries) create in your body.**

When you reward your child or grandchild with a bag of french fries, it takes over three months (102 days) for it to be properly processed through the body. During that time period, the body does not have adequate fat production, which jeopardizes nerve transmission. **Improper nerve function is one of the primary reasons that we have hyperactivity in our society.** Adding to the diet essential fats like flax oil with proper minerals and B vitamins can result in a dramatic reduction of hyperactivity.

The half-life for the Omega 3 fat, or cis fat is 18 days. That is why it may take three weeks before you notice improvement once implementing this program. We start the program with one salmon oil capsule per night for the first 18 days. Salmon oil is a direct source of Omega 3 fat and, unlike flax, does not need to be synthesized with B6, Zinc and Magnesium. I do not want to continue salmon oil use daily after 18 days. This may result in an imbalance and other problems.

The Problem with Cow's Milk

Cow's milk has been a part of man's diet for years and contains hundreds of different fatty acids. Bacteria in one of the cow's four stomachs destroys essential fatty acids by hydrogenating (saturating) them. For this reason, *cow's milk is almost always low in essential fatty acids.* In recently released research, a milk protein called "casomorphin" has been linked as a possible cause of ADHD. Americans consume over 30 pounds of cheese a year.

A testimonial of the effects of dairy foods is from David, who was having behavioral challenges. My wife, Debbie, explained our program to his mom. **David's mother eliminated dairy and added flax to his diet.** Two weeks into the modification he started to improve. Adding dairy to his diet once again aggravated his disposition. The family is now dairy free and using flax as a supplement. David is showing great success with no drugs.

Says David's mom, "I introduced David to flax oil at Dr. DeMaria's suggestion. David is in fifth grade and has approximately an hour of homework at night. This hour had become four or five hours because David was having trouble concentrating on one thing. David was also having difficulty getting up in the morning. By the end of the first week of flax consumption, he was a completely different child. I tried my own experiment and stopped the flax after two weeks. The change was amazing! He went right back to sleeping longer, taking twice as long with homework, and ignoring all of his chores. He is now back on flax and I have tried to cut as much dairy out of his diet as possible. In all, his behavior has improved immensely."

As a clinician, I am also concerned about the chemicals in the food fed to dairy cattle today, the drugs given to them to survive and the artificially forced lactation. *MY PATIENTS REPORT PAIN RELIEF WITH THE REDUCTION OF DAIRY PRODUCTS*. Patients who have a variety of functional problems— including asthma, sinus, hay fever, digestive problems, joint pain, and hyperactivity— ALWAYS get better without dairy. Non-milk drinkers don't necessarily get osteoporosis or have weak bones either. Don't be fooled by slick marketing campaigns.

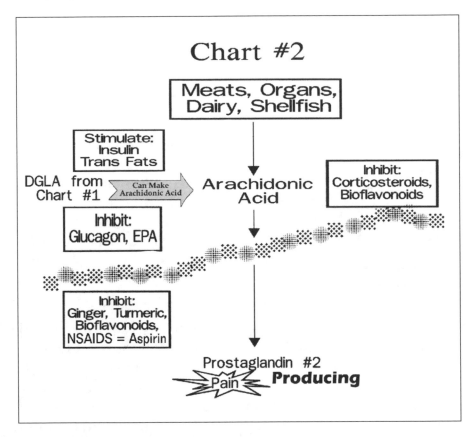

Look at Chart #2. **Arachidonic acid,** which is a **pain-producing fat** and **blood cell sticking fat,** may have its production *increased by insulin*. Insulin is elevated by sugar and carbohydrate consumption. **Production of arachidonic acid can also be increased in volume by the** *consumption of transfatty acids, causing an imbalance.* **The production of this fat can be**

inhibited by steroids like cortisone and bioflavonoids contained in fresh fruit sources and fish oil.

Today we consume less "good" oil and fat in our diets than 20 years ago, and consume more "bad" oil and fat. (This is the subject of constant debate and can be confusing to some people.) Research by many professionals, including the author of *Eat Fat – Lose Weight*, Ann Louise Gittleman, has shown that oil/fat called conjugated linoleic acid (CLA) sourced from animal and vegetable oils, is helpful in burning fat. Reduction of its intake may be a reason for obesity, nervous system dysfunction, and other health problems. I agree that we do eat less "good" fat (almonds, walnuts, cashews, avocados and coconut), which contributes to our society's health woes, including obesity and chronic hyperactivity.

I personally believe the real issue is not more EPA and DHA from direct sources, but normalization of fat synthesis that has been interrupted by hydrogenated fat consumption.

I encourage my patients to be aware of their consumption of the "good" fats: corn, sunflower, borage, safflower and primrose oils. I coach them to monitor their consumption of red meat, organs, dairy and shellfish, in order to balance their consumption of fat. How often do you think of flax (an Omega 3 fat precursor) or other oils as beneficial?

Eicosapentaenoic Acid (EPA) and Docosahexaenoic Acid (DHA) are two very important Omega 3 fatty acids for nervous system, brain health and pain relief. EPA and DHA can also be obtained from the oils of cold-water fish and marine animals. I personally believe the real issue is not more EPA and DHA from direct sources, but normalization of fat synthesis that has been interrupted by hydrogenated fat consump- tion. Information suggests DHA from animal foods may be the key to solving modern neurological problems, but clinically I do not see this being a viable alternative for the long haul. There are many reasons why animal sources are not the best choices. They often contain toxins, and processed marine food and farmed marine food may not have the same value as seafood from nature. Fat from plants contain the precursors of EFAs while animal fats contain the derivatives. The derivatives of the EFAs can produce physiological changes faster than EFAs found in vegetables. Stubborn cases may need continued supplementation of cold-water fish oils and marine foods. Generally, with flax oil, adequate B vitamins and minerals have proven successful.

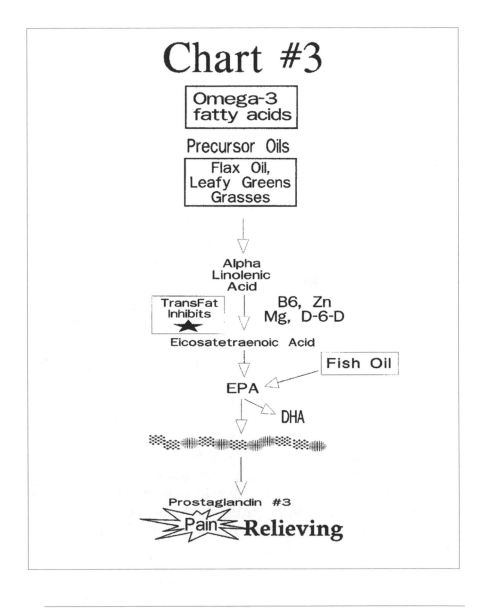

Chart #3 shows how the body manufactures prostaglandin #3, which requires as its primary source flaxseed oil, leafy greens and grasses. Consuming flax oil alone, in capsules or liquid, makes a huge difference in my patients. Hyperactivity and other chronic health challenges, (i.e., flaky skin, eczema, headaches, back pain, bowel problems, asthma, etc.) will respond to flaxseed supplementation.

These precursor foods (flax oil, leafy greens and grasses) must go through similar steps as prostaglandin #1. These steps can be hindered when adequate B6, zinc, D-6-D and magnesium are not included in the diet. Sugar consumption depletes the body of these elements and they are also inhibited by hydrogenated fats and food additives. Americans often have an imbalance of fats with not enough of the prostaglandin #3. Prior to World War II, most people ate a ratio of one to one with one part of prostaglandin #1 and #2 foods and one part prostaglandin #3 food. This ratio maintained a balance of Omega 3 fats and Omega 6 fats.

Various opinions have been released in reference to the Omega 6 and Omega 3 ratio. I have seen "normal" ratios suggested as 1 to 1 up to 4 to 1. Our current eating patterns create an imbalance in this ratio.

Edward N. Siguel, M.D., Ph. D., in his book *Essential Fatty Acids in Health & Disease*, states, "Many children also have Omega 3 deficiencies that effect their mental abilities, therefore it is very important to learn to eat a balanced mixture of Omega 3 and Omega 6 fatty acids starting in childhood." Dr. Siguel continued by making a general statement, "that since most textbooks do not discuss deficiencies, it is not recognized in the U.S. as a problem. In my research I have found that the bodies of most people can manufacture the Omega 3 fats found in fish oils from the EFA linolenic acid obtained from vegetable oils. **Because eating fish oils over long periods of time may cause undesirable complications in some people, fish oils should be used for only a short period of time until vegetable oils begin to have and effect.**"

I hope these charts illustrate important information and may show why you and your family may need to make lifestyle changes. Many conditions can result because of poor/improper fat metabolism.

Elimination of sugar alone may not always alter hyperactivity in a child because there may be a problem with fat metabolism facilitated by eating snack foods and foods fried with hydrogenated fats. Consuming milk, cheese and all dairy (pizza, macaroni and cheese) can create a fat metabolism imbalance (due to the arachidonic acid in the dairy). (Refer to chart #2). Consuming processed low fat, high sugar foods and drinking soda pop which contains up to 9 1/2 teaspoons of sugar per can creates imbalance. Sugar depletes B vitamins, Zinc (Zn) and magnesium (Mg), which are essential components explored in Fact #2. There are three basic factors leading to the problem:

☑ **Sugar**

☑ **Dairy**

☑ **Hydrogenated Fats.**

Here are the results of my son, Jesse 9 years old and my daughter, Alicia 7 years old, while on Dr. Bob's program.

Jesse complained less and was less hyper. He was not as emotional. He cried less and had fewer headaches. There were no dark circles under his eyes and fewer sore throats. He had more energy, a more positive attitude, better school performance and slept better.

Alicia had less whining, crying, moping and sadness. There was less "tickle" in her throat and decreased complaining of small hurts. She had more smiles, positive attitude, more energy, better school performance and got out of bed easier in the morning for school.

Needless to say, mommy was HAPPIER!

EPA and DHA synthesis from
plant source precursor food
is necessary for optimal long term
behavorial function.

Keep in mind the half-life of transfatty acids or
hydrogenated fats is 51 days.
This means that it takes your body 51 days to
process these fats to reduce them to half
strength and another 51 days for this process to
continue on. It takes at least 102 days to minimize
the negative effects it does to your body.

Improper fat metabolism is the number one reason
your child is in an unhealthy neurological state.
"Essential Fatty Acids" are necessary for the
transmission of electrical impulses.

Hydrogenated fats, i.e., transfatty acids, snack
food fats, convenience food fats, inhibit the
transmission of essential brain information.

5

Fact #2:
Sugar Consumption

Sugar Depletes Essential Minerals and Vitamins
Necessary For Proper Fat Metabolism

Not too long ago, cakes, cookies and candy were an exclusive treat mostly for celebratory occasions. Today, sugar invades 95 percent of our canned and processed foods. Sweets are no longer for celebratory occasions, but instead for every occasion.

Cookies, cakes, candy and pop are fun foods. They are attractive foods, beautifully decorated and have interesting flavors, but they offer more problems to our health.

This leads to our second fact: **sugar depletes the body of essential minerals and B vitamins.** You and your family are probably eating too much sugar and this is another direct link to hyperactivity and other problems.

You and your family are consuming too much sugar. Why do we have a deficiency of the essential nutrients, including B6, zinc, magnesium and other important minerals? The answer to that is very simply put: You and your family are consuming too much sugar.

All sugar, whether natural or refined, requires B-complex vitamins, calcium, and magnesium for digestion. Complex carbohydrates, such as fruits, vegetables and starches, contain enough of these nutrients to assist our bodies in their own digestion. However, simple, refined sugars (like white and brown) do not assist our bodies. Therefore, the body must call upon its own reserves of these nutrients in order to digest this kind of sugar. **B-complex is taken from the nervous system, and calcium and magnesium are robbed from the bones and teeth when these sugars are consumed.** "Consequently," observes Dr. Tessler in the book *Healthy Habits*, "refined sugar 'rips you off' of these needed nutrients, resulting in 'raw' nerves."

With a steady loss of calcium and magnesium from our bones and teeth, osteoporosis is a likely outcome. Once the bones and skeletal structure begin to soften, minerals are released in the body where they settle and accumulate in the joints, causing a condition known as arthritis.

Effect of Sugar on White Blood Cell Activity

Amount of Refined Sugar Consumed	The Number of Bacteria a WBC Can Process in ½ Hour	Decrease in Immunity
No Sugar	14	0%
6 tsp. = 8 oz of soft drink	10	25%
12 tsp. = frosted brownie	5.5	60%
18 tsp. = apple pie a'la mode	2	85%
24 tsp. = banana split	1	92%
Uncontrolled Diabetic	1	92%

Table courtesy of Dr. David Frohm

(Special Note: A 12-ounce can of soda contains 9 teaspoons of sugar. An 8-ounce serving of fruit-flavored yogurt contains almost as much.)

Sugar impairs the functioning of your immune system. The previous chart shows how refined sugar weakens white blood cells. White blood cells are essential to your state of health; they eat-up foreign invaders and seek and destroy cancerous cells. When sugar is consumed, your immune system is weakened. You and your family will "get sick" and require antibiotics. This begins the downward spiral of poor health. Flu season starts in America around Halloween and continues through into the spring (Easter candy). The "flu bug" is not necessarily an invader. You have various "bugs" in you. When you consume sugar, your immune system is weakened. The unfriendly "critters" take over and you get sick. Not all people "catch" the flu. Patients in my practice who understand this *DO NOT GET SICK*.

9½ teaspoons of sugar

> Digestion is critical in maintaining B12 levels,
> proper fat metabolism, and clean blood vessels.

NOTES:

6

Fact #3: Parasites

What came first?
The parasite or hyperactivity?

Parasites Can be Part of Your Child's Problem

We often think of parasites living everywhere else but within our bodies. If the body is not running at its optimum level it becomes more susceptible to parasites. So, what is a parasite? A parasite is an organism that is receiving food and shelter at the expense of another organism. It has been estimated that 85 percent of the North American adult population has at least one form of parasite living in their body. Their presence often mimics other, more familiar diseases like the flu, therefore making them difficult to detect.

How can a parasite live inside my body without my knowing it? This is easy! The purpose of a parasite is to make itself unknown. A smart parasite lives without being detected because if discovered, it will be eradicated by the body. They are highly intelligent organisms in their ability to survive and reproduce. Do you suffer from parasite infestation? "Parasitic infections are a major cause of illness in the United States," stated Dr. Theodore Nash from the National Institute of Allergy and Infectious Diseases (Bethesda, Maryland) in a 1993 press release. We may be living longer but we are certainly not living healthier. Parasites may be one contributing factor to the deterioration of our health.

Why are parasites becoming an increasing problem? Travel to tropical countries means we are exposed to a greater variety and number of parasitic organisms through contaminated food and water. The parasites can be carried in or on imported foods and quickly passed to other foods. Parasites, like other creatures, have an eliminating process, meaning they "go to the bathroom" in the host (you). Part of the challenge is that the parasites release toxins into your body, poisons that our bodies are forced to address by increasing the process of detoxification.

When the diet and the environment threaten the parasite inhabitation, they will leave. If we have secretions from parasites and create our own toxic overload by drinking alcohol, smoking cigarettes, eating junk food, and breathing polluted air, the extra stress and strain on the body's cleansing system can be enough to push the body into toxic overload. Remember, sugar consumption alters digestion. Without proper enzymes, acid forms in the digestive system and creates an environment for parasites to flourish. Again, you need to clean the machine to have a body that works to its optimum level.

Through nutritional microscopy, I often see hyperactive individuals who have unfriendly bacteria or parasites in their body. If your child is taking Ritalin, have them checked for parasitic infestation. Some common body signals of individuals with pin worms are:

☑ thrashing in bed

☑ tearing the bed apart

☑ grinding the teeth

☑ challenges falling asleep

☑ not resting well

☑ often craving very high carbohydrate foods

☑ and sometimes salt, sugar and pizza

In my experience, I have seen individuals with parasites also suffer from yeast infestation. This may be a reason why pizza/bread is "craved!" A simple test called the "Saliva Test" can be performed. Generally, if you have a positive test, you more than likely have parasites and yeast.

Saliva Test

To check for yeast use this test:

First thing in the morning, before brushing teeth, eating or drinking anything, spit into a glass of cold water. If the saliva goes to the bottom of the glass, whether in a long string(s) or bunches up and drops to the bottom in a ball, candida is present in the system. If the saliva stays afloat on the top of the glass, the candida is gone.

An unhealthy body is conducive to parasites' survival. Will parasites go away on their own? **When you minimize sugar and yeast-based food consumption and have proper oil in your body, these unfriendly creatures will leave.** Understand that human beings do have parasitic involvement; this is part of the natural eco-system. We have bacteria in our bodies. However, you can have a health challenges when you have an over-abundance and/or a form of these creatures that have toxins which are released from their own metabolism. You will need to decide if your pets contribute to any parasitic contamination. Your pet (especially cats) may need to be treated or removed from the premises while your child is going through this transition.

You could still be at risk if you do not own a pet. Parasites can be transmitted from child to child at day care centers. Parasites can be lodged under fingernails. Be aware that poor hygiene is still very prevalent in the United States and your child may have infestations due to contaminates from playmates as well as animals. Think of the numerous ways we have contact with others: the bus, stores, restaurants and playgrounds (especially the colorful vats of plastic balls kids enjoy jumping into).

When handling any type of raw meat product, game or domestic, certain precautions should be observed to reduce the likelihood of contamination or infection. Generally precautions include maintaining a clean food preparation surface, the use of protective gloves, and thoroughly washing your hands. This is most important if you are preparing wild game.

Parasitic involvement **must be looked into if the body signals are apparent** (thrashing in bed, etc.) I am not saying the symptoms are exclusively caused by parasites, but it's best parasites be ruled out.

The optimal internal environment must be maintained or the "critters" will return. I have seen it take from three months to five years to control the parasite overgrowth. It does not change if the parties involved are not willing to make necessary lifestyle modifications, including pet relocation.

> Eight of 51 children had daily dietary intakes that were less than 67 percent of the RDA for iron, zinc and energy.

7

Fact #4:
Vitamin B-Complex Deficiency Syndrome

Avoid The Greatest Nutritional Deficiency in America: B-Complex Deficiency Syndrome

B vitamin deficiency symptoms exist in nearly all patients I see daily. Recently we have seen a number of job-loss, stress-related problems. A particular patient came into my office near the breaking point. She was shaking, depressed, lethargic, exhausted and dizzy. Her primary stressors were that she was a single mom with a son, had a father in ill health and had experienced the recent death of her mother. She was physically and emotionally exhausted with depleted vitamin B reserves. We supplemented her with whole food B vitamins and within one week she was stable. I urgently reminded her about limiting sugar, which accelerates B vitamin use in the body. Most Americans have a major stress factor in their life precipitating the B vitamin Deficiency Syndrome.

One of the most common nutritional deficiencies and most commonly misdiagnosed problems in America is **B-Complex Deficiency Syndrome (BCDS)**. This is because most doctors feel either that vitamin deficiencies are a lot of bunk or that "enriched" processed foods fill nutritional voids. Lots of bogus diagnoses are given to people suffering from a simple deficiency of B vitamins. Some of the most common are:

- ☑ Hyperactivity
- ☑ Hypoglycemia
- ☑ Candidiasis
- ☑ Premenstrual syndrome
- ☑ Neuritis, neuralgia
- ☑ Depression

The Real Diagnosis

B-Complex Deficiency Syndrome will not be found in any medical diagnosis textbook. That is particularly sad since this condition is rampant in America. What you will find in medical texts—including *BioChemistry* (Kleiner and Orten), *Principles of BioChemistry* (White, Handler, Smith, and Stetton), *Textbook of Medicine* (Cecil), and *Rehabilitation Through Better Nutrition* (Tom Spies, MD) is an abundance of data about BCDS.

Some of the symptoms of BCDS (as found in the textbooks) are:

- ☑ Weakness and fatigue
- ☑ Indigestion (hypochlorhydria)
- ☑ Poor appetite
- ☑ Craving for sweets
- ☑ Neuralgia and neuritis
- ☑ Muscular soreness
- ☑ Headache
- ☑ Insomnia
- ☑ Dizziness
- ☑ Nervousness
- ☑ Instability
- ☑ Forgetfulness
- ☑ Vague fears
- ☑ Uneasiness
- ☑ Rage
- ☑ Hostility
- ☑ Depression
- ☑ Anxiety
- ☑ Apprehension

B-Vitamin Complex

It's not easy to get real B vitamins in the American diet. First of all, the richest source of these vitamins is brewer's yeast (not exactly a staple of the average American's diet). Other rich sources include liver and whole grain cereals. (Speaking of cereals, don't fall for fake commercials about needing four bowls of another cereal to get the vitamin equivalent of one bowl of "enriched" cereal.) **No amount of synthetic B-vitamin fractions added to food will substitute for the real B-complex as found in nature.**

BCDS Becomes Chronic

When you suffer from B-vitamin deficiency over a long period, undue stress is placed upon the adrenal glands, which give you the ability to cope with stress. As long as your adrenal glands can put out sufficient adrenal hormone, you will survive BCDS. But when adrenal function can no longer compensate, watch out! See adrenal gland page 13.

The Adrenal Gland Connection

Weakening adrenal function in the presence of starvation for B vitamins causes about *half* of all the lower back pain in America! Continued weakening of the adrenals leads to heart decomposition and heart problems, potentially even heart attacks. And when adrenal malfunction nears the critical stage, (hyperactivity, ADD, ADHD, ODD) nervous exhaustion occurs, with the potential for a full-blown nervous breakdown.

Don't Wait for Disaster

Don't court disaster by treating conditions like hypoglycemia, candidiasis, premenstrual syndrome and others with drugs or fad diets. Instead, alter your diet to include foods rich in vitamin B. If whole grain foods aren't enough, get a quality whole food vitamin B complex supplement (3-6 tablets daily).

What to Expect from Healthful Nutrition

If you start a nutritional supplement program, be aware that after a few days to a week on the program, unusual or increased fatigue or even exhaustion is common. This increased fatigue results from repair mechanisms within your body. It is proof positive that your program is working. Such fatigue is usually short-lived and self-limiting.

Within 30 days you will begin feeling much better. But remember, to completely recover from BCDS takes time. If you have already advanced to the stage of severe depression, fear, insomnia and the like, it may require a few months to begin to see improvement and it may take a year or longer to completely recover.

A deficient diet—a nonfood diet—depletes energy, leading to a lack of activity and isolation and eventually depression.

8

Surviving Other Factors

Improper fat metabolism and sugar consumption are crucial contributors to hyperactivity and your child's impaired state of health. Since hyperactivity is a booming "syndrome" in America, various theories prefer to explain the cause. Even though the following theories are possible contributors to the cause of hyperactivity, **remember: we could have a million theories, a thousand drugs, but the answer is to be health conscious, not drugged into complacency.**

Immunizations

The early part of the twentieth century saw hundreds of children dying from Whooping Cough. In 1912, two French bacteriologists, Jules Bordet and Octave Gengou, created the first whooping cough vaccine. The intent behind a vaccine is to artificially induce immunity against a specific disease. In the United States, children have 20 different immunizations by the age of two.

Hyperactivity has been linked to the DPT vaccine, specifically the "P," pertussis.

Hyperactivity has been linked to the DPT vaccine, specifically the "P," pertussis. Children who have a negative reaction to the vaccine often exhibit signs of mal convulsions, spitting-up breast-milk, high fever, and arching the back while screaming.

Some of the symptoms that surface later in life are:

☑ upper respiratory infection

☑ exhibiting signs of a "slow learner," (cannot complete a project, confused, not being able to cope with simple tasks)

☑ allergy to milk

☑ ear infections

☑ short attention span

☑ inability to concentrate

☑ poor memory

☑ hyperactivity

☑ sleep disturbances.

You may notice that some of the symptoms are found in a hyperactive child. Could the two be interrelated? Presently, there is no viable information that links the DPT vaccine to hyperactivity. However, the high mercury content needed to bond multiple vaccinations has been suspected in causing seizure disorders and autism.

Vaccinations may precipitate a series of negative side effects, including hyperactivity and ADD. What is frustrating to parents is that some states have mandatory immunizations or a child faces suspension from school. Some states even set up vaccine booths at shopping plazas.

Lead Poisoning

A publication from the EPA about lead poisoning states, "You may have lead around your building without knowing it, because you can't see, taste or smell lead. You may have lead in the dust, paint or soil in and around your home, or in your drinking water or food." Lead has been used in paint, water pipes, gasoline and many other products.

Hyperactivity and learning disabilities are long-term effects associated with lead poisoning.

Hyperactivity and learning disabilities are long-term effects associated with lead poisoning. Your child may have come in contact with lead through paint chips, water from old pipes, or mother may have had lead poisoning during pregnancy.

There are numerous steps to take for prevention beginning with having your home and water tested for lead contamination. The most important thing to do is maintain a healthy diet. The more iron, calcium and zinc a child has in his/her diet, the less lead is absorbed. That means your child should be eating leafy green vegetables, eggs, beans and nuts.

The Mother's Health

A child does not enter this world disaffected by the mother's health nor by the birth process. If the mother ate a diet high in trans fats and sugar, then the child's health is disrupted from conception. The mother's food choices, smoking and drinking habits influenced the cellular formation of the child. An unhealthy mother guarantees an unhealthy child.

Cesarean sections are becoming more commonplace today than twenty years ago. The reasoning behind this could be the "ease" for doctors to perform a cesarean section vs. the time consuming, more personal, vaginal birth. This, too, can affect the child's state of health.

Candida, or yeast can cause hormone imbalances. The overgrowth of yeast can be traced back to the birth process. Donna Gates, the author of *The Body Ecology Diet*, states, "Up until birth, when we are living inside our mothers, we live in a very sterile environment. Then we pass through the birth canal and we're exposed for the first time to the bacteria in the outside world. The mother literally inoculates her baby with these beneficial bacteria that will develop into the baby's immune system. The immune system begins in the gut and it begins at birth. Many people become susceptible to candida overgrowth because they are not inoculated with the right bacteria at birth." Therefore, with cesarean sections, the child is not given the opportunity to strengthen his/her immune system.

Birth Order

The second child has the "potential" to develop various health-related problems from a mother who would be depleted of essential vitamins, minerals and precious fats. The mother, more than likely, will have a congested liver from working overtime to protect the first baby from getting unwanted toxins. I have noticed an unusual number of second children who have "facial" freckles around the nose and below the eyes that will disappear with liver cleansing. The liver is the primary organ for proper fat metabolism in the body. A congested liver will result in a lower state of health.

Once again, we see that every influence between the mother and child eventually surfaces and affects the child.

Familial Situation

Today we are forced to redefine the meaning of family. There are divorced couples, "step" family members, co-habitating partners, children raised by aging grandparents, latchkey kids, and many children, who have parents who are emotionally indifferent, raising themselves. With the rise in scattered families comes a parallel rise in hyperactivity.

Children mimic behavior they witness at home. If a child does not see stability, but is entranced by the "drama" and violence of television or family, then that child will mimic those behaviors in and out of school.

Socially, we Americans are left to wander within a society that minimizes showing of affection, discourages talk about emotions and feelings, and has lost the concept of unconditional give-and-take of relationships.

If a child is hyperactive, distracted and violent, then the child's influences must be evaluated. How much time does your family spend together? How much time do you spend talking about your day? How often do you cook together? How often does your child experience affection within the home? These are all crucial components in a child's life. A child grows stress-free with affection and discourse, not by yelling or through a television.

Communicate with the Teacher

Children may be pushed into a hyperactive/ADD/ADHD/ODD diagnosis due to activity in the classroom. Teachers in today's school systems have been forced into a position of referee rather than educator. Students charged up on breakfast food may not ever settle down during the school day. You need to have open communication with the teacher, parents and counselors, discussing option before medication is initiated.

Often, a child may exhibit hyperactive behavior in the classroom due to simple boredom. Video games and TV have our children programmed to recognize fast, colorful, stimulating environments and at subconscious levels. How is this information presented to them? Are there too many students per classroom?

> **Often, a child may exhibit hyperactive behavior in the classroom due to simple boredom... Don't automatically label your child as hyperactive before evaluating his/her circumstances.**

Don't automatically label your child as hyperactive before evaluating his/her circumstances. Make your own assessment. Sometimes it may be wise for you to obtain a tutor or simply spend extra time with your child. Some parents are disconnected from their kid's life.

Doctors

When visiting with a doctor, it is always important to remember that he/she will not know your child better than you. The doctor does not have the final word, but in some instances in the past, parents had little choice when their children were taken away. Children services had been called into a family environment of one of my patients and threatened to take her child if he was not put on medication immediately. Remember that doctors feel they are under pressure by pharmaceutical companies, time restraints within the office, and they know that the more Ritalin/Clonidine/Paxil they prescribe, the more money they get from insurance companies and HMO's. This is reality.

Doctors often spend no more than ten minutes with a child. Often they do not evaluate the child's diet, the family environment or the school environment. Everything your child does, sees, hears and eats directly influences his/her perception and behavior, and your doctor may not spend the time to determine these factors.

> More than 80 percent of the amphetamine use in the USA, according to the DEA, is for treatment of hyperactivity/ADHD/ADD/ODD.

9
Hitting the Hype:
You are What You Eat

My research suggests kids who are hyperactive eat foods that are processed, devitalized and loaded with sugar, hydrogenated fats and dairy. Because many of today's parents both work and schedules are hectic, they are pushed into a time crunch: no time to shop, no time to cook and no time to eat properly. Processed convenience food has become a big business. Everything is packaged and made easy for people on the run. So why not take up the challenge to be creative by cooking with fresh food?

Prepackaged, canned, **cellophane-wrapped food** should be your last choice. However, starting a program of eating healthy must be done in steps; immediate upheaval of your lifestyle will cause failure.

To begin, establish choices and priorities. Start with a "wholesome breakfast" at home. Then proceed with packed lunches; maybe not daily at first, but on a regular basis. Think of the cost of convenience foods (restaurants, school lunches, vending machines and drive-throughs). Compare this with what foods you buy for in-home preparation. You will find that you are beginning to save money while avoiding foods that provide minimal or no living whole-food nutrient complexes. You will begin to understand why healthy families and children eat at home.

You may wonder about manufacturers who enrich foods with vital nutrients, what I call "media nutrients" because they are promoted by media. For example, calcium and potassium are the latest "media nutrients." Think of promotions for orange juice and margarine with extra calcium. If you eat organic fresh fruits and vegetables, your dependence on "enriched foods" would decrease. Nature did not make nutrient-deficient foods. Man created it for shelf longevity. Dr. Braly emphasizes the complexities of shelf longevity and devitalized foods:

"Feeling as I do that many behavioral problems are traceable in large measure to food allergies and the American diet, it seems to me a travesty of responsible parenthood and citizenship that we allow our food supply to be laden with common food allergens and poisoned by chemicals, and then tout this food to our children via children's television programs."

Americans consume more than 20 pounds of snack food every year.

"Media nutrients" influence our choices by misleading us with flashy marketing schemes that sell their products while depriving us from healthy eating.

The American Food Pyramid – The Great American Lie

Recently, I was at our local hospital cafeteria with a friend. As I looked around the cafeteria, I observed that most of the staff and customers were overweight, limping, waddling from obesity and in generally pitiful shape. I was overwhelmed by the absence of proper food, as well as the preponderance of over-cooked food. Nearly all these individuals were consuming Jell-O (basically hardened sugar water with dyes). Ironically, the foods that lead to poor health is served in hospitals! Are you shocked? What are dieticians doing?

Look on a box of cereal, crackers or in any grocery store and the food pyramid catches your attention. You could probably recite it's structure from memory, but do you live your life by it? Subconsciously, you may do a checklist of which area of the food pyramid you've consumed.

The American food pyramid was created in 1992, with the intent to "guide" the scattered diets of modern Americans. There are two troubling components of the American food pyramid:

1. the types of fats and oils to be used "sparingly" is vague,

2. meat, poultry, and fish are grouped with beans, nuts, and eggs. Healthy oils and fats are disregarded to promote a low-fat diet.

To be a health-conscious person carefully read labels. Recognize which foods utilize the American Food Pyramid to promote their products. A leading breakfast toaster pastry utilizes the American Food Pyramid to promote this product as a "good source of 7 vitamins and minerals." This type of labeling is misguiding because a consumer may disregard the ingredients to instead follow the food pyramid guide. When we look at the ingredients of the toaster pastry we see: strawberry filling, corn syrup, dextrose, high fructose corn syrup, partially hydrogenated soy bean oil, enriched wheat flour, sugar, gelatin and coloring. Just these main ingredients contribute to the "peak" of the American Food Pyramid.

> **Food manufacturers are marketing a food that *seemingly* belongs to the bread and cereal group, but actually is composed of trans fats and sugar. Parents are fooled into believing that they are offering a healthy breakfast while contributing to their child's diminished state of health.**

Be aware that the "nutrition facts" delineated on the label are for one serving. Notice how much of what is in one serving. It may be one item, or ounces or gram sizes. The manufacturers will try to present their product to be consumer friendly. You may have a large container that has several servings. Consuming the entire product may give you more than what you bargained for—you think you are only getting the amount on the label for one serving but the product has more than one serving in the package.

Food manufactures try to confuse consumers. This is why being ingredient savvy will contribute to your family's improved state of health. Why would anyone follow a food pyramid that contributes to heart disease, obesity and hyperactivity? You will need to become well versed in reading these labels. Do not be fooled by what food manufactures are trying to slip by you. Christine Hoza Farlow, D.C., in her guide "Food Additives, A Shopper's Guide to What is Safe and What is Not," states:

> *"Often the package has statements like 'natural fruit flavors with real fruit juice' or 'all natural ingredients and no preservatives added.' This does not mean there are no harmful additives in the product. The manufacturer hopes you'll think these are healthy, natural products...if the list of ingredients is long, there's probably a lot of chemical additives in the product, and you're risking your health by eating it. If the list of ingredients is short, it may or may not have harmful additives. So read the ingredients carefully before you decide to purchase the product."*

When more processed food is consumed than whole food, there is imbalance within the body.

We consume far too many man-made foods containing added chemicals. **When more processed food is consumed than whole food, there is imbalance within the body.** Consistency is a crucial diet component that should be applied to all areas of life. An individual will have an imbalance of health if too many processed foods are consumed including saturated fats, dairy and meat. (See the "Transition Chart" on page 88.) There are food groups to avoid and food groups that are more acceptable in promoting health. I encourage a diet consisting of 75 percent raw or steamed vegetables and grains and 25 percent meats and nuts.

I know with the reality of time, budget, tastes and lifestyle that you will not be "perfect" all the time. You may only hit the balance half of the time. Your goal is more whole, organic, acceptable and vital foods. Consuming processed foods deplete your body's enzymes and nutrients that are necessary for tissue repair and vitalization. It takes more whole organic food to counterbalance the negative effects of chemically treated food items.

Fast Food: A Link to Hyperactivity

Fast food is tempting; it's everywhere. But it is avoidable. You don't save money by eating at these places, and you aren't nourishing yourself or your child.

If you demand healthier food, fast food restaurants will eventually serve healthier foods.

If you demand healthier food, fast food restaurants will eventually serve healthier foods. (Recently, McDonald's surprised the public by reducing the amount of transfatty acids in their top secret french fry formula.) If you demand nut seed shakes and spritzers, fast food restaurants will accommodate. It is up to the American population to spark a revolution and redefine fast foods, it is starting.

Fast food is a staple in the diet of the rushed American. It offers the comforts of convenience and decent taste yet little commitment. Eric Schlosser, in his book *Fast Food Nation*, states, "The typical American consumes about three hamburgers and four orders of french fries every week. Roughly a quarter of the nation's population buys fast foods every day." During America's morning commute, many commuters pass through McDonalds or Burger King. We have vending machines to motivate us through our day. Convenience is the key; it's easy and satisfying.

Have you ever noticed how much of your food is flawless and uniform in appearance? French fries go through a more thorough examination than you do during a visit to your doctor. Schlosser states,

> *"Conveyor belts took the wet, clean potatoes into a machine that blasted them with steam for twelve seconds, boiled the water under their skins and exploded the skins off. Four video cameras scrutinize them from different angles, looking for flaws...Men and women in white coats analyzed french fries all day and night, measuring their sugar content, their starch content, their color."*

Your french fries are made in a laboratory setting. They are altered by added sugars, oils and colorings (providing the golden brown coloring). What is more threatening is that these laboratory fries are then fried in hydrogenated oil. Eating these types of foods four times a week—ingesting it's synthetic properties and hydrogenated oils—**is what is causing an unhealthy body and an epidemic of hyperactive children.**

The old saying goes: "You are what you eat." If so, you're part laboratory french fry and part contaminated meats. Normally, cattle are fed grain and permitted to roam freely. But for the fast food industry, time is money and the more beef produced, the more money is made. Due to the rise in grain prices, cattle are fed high-protein foods, including other animals. Millions of dead cats and dead dogs, purchased from animal shelters, are being fed to cattle each year. We had a wake up call at the beginning of 2001 with Foot and Mouth Disease. We need to evaluate how our food is produced. When you order a hamburger know you are also getting pieces of other animals. But you would never think of your fast food that way; fast food suggests family and fun. Start thinking!

Sharp marketing campaigns attract children faster than adults. Children are lured to the food via the toy associated with a "happy meal." Children see only the glitz and thrill of the toy, unaware that consuming unhealthy food will lead to their unhealthy future. Advertising companies are apparently unconcerned that, by attracting children to big fast food chains, they are contributing to the systematic poisoning of America's children by their clients.

Fast food does not always come from restaurants. Vending machines are a relatively new vehicle for distributing fast snack foods to school kids. Because funding for schools are so limited, Coca-Cola and Pepsi exchange funding for the marketing of their product. Schools then can upgrade computer labs, celebrate certain holidays and have extra amenities due to the funds provided by the "super" snack food providers.

School kids now have access to junk food before school, between classes and after school. This means adding more sugar and empty calories to already unhealthy bodies. This promotes Type 2 diabetes and may enhance a child's hyperactive state. Combining processed, devitalized foods with junk food leaves little change for school kids to grow into healthy, aware adults. The next time your child's school has a new score board or computer lab, think about the risks taken to obtain those items.

Parents in New York were so angered by the funding from "corporate food factories" that they sued the New York Board of Education. (Recently in California vending machines are being removed from schools.) An agreement was reached and now New York schools can sell only nutritious snacks during lunch hour. This should be an example to everyone. We do have the power to change our systems for the better. If children have access to unhealthy food, then they will become unhealthy adults suffering from chronic physical ailments. Who wants to be 25 years old and feel 75 years old? Lets help our children to see the beauty of optimal health!

If children have access to unhealthy food, then they will become unhealthy adults suffering from chronic physical ailments.

The Low-Fat Myth

Although fast food restaurants have made unsuccessful attempts to cater to the low-fat craze, convenience foods have fueled this craze. These foods still maintain their attractive appeal by promoting the illusion of weight loss. After many years of consuming these foods, have you seen any weight loss?

Americans—with the encouragement of well-meaning but ill-informed physicians and nutrition advisors—are on a low-fat craze. Yet, Americans become more unhealthy. Low-fat diets, combined with other factors, produce a syndrome that is rapidly becoming epidemic. Obesity, abnormal liver function with high cholesterol and triglyceride levels, elevated levels of insulin, a predisposition to blood clotting, hormonal imbalances and the tendency of all these factors to combine to choke off the blood vessels that feed the heart and brain. This may be a factor for the rise in the number of strokes among those under sixty.

What is the most common health problem for Americans despite 10 to 15 years of consuming low-fat foods? The answer is clogged arteries and heart disease. The solution to these problems is not a low-fat diet. This has become a cruel hoax in medical circles. Here's why:

1. The medical media has infused in us that a diet low in fat is best. Fully eight percent of school children now think that the healthiest diet is one that eliminates *all fat*—a death sentence diet.

2. Studies prove that eating less fat causes the body to make more fat at a dramatically increased rate, which is then stored more easily. So eating low fat will cause more fat. And, unlike the clinical studies proving this fact, there is *no proof at all* that eating a higher-fat diet causes obesity.

3. Oxidation (cell breakdown) of fats can cause cancer. *Saturated fats*, like meat and dairy, do not oxidize easily. Fully 41 percent of all physicians polled were

under the mistaken belief that saturated fats were the oxidation culprits in cancer. The fact is fake fats and low-fat concoctions are the real culprits: just read the ingredients on a can of Pringles.

4. Along with an Omega 3 fat supplement (like a tablespoon of raw flax oil) for two to three years, consumption of **monounsaturated fat** (olive oil) must also be part of the diet. That's why I recommend extra-virgin, first-pressed olive oil for salads dressings, food preparation and cooking. If oxidation of fats acts like **rusting** in your body, *olive oil is Rustoleum*.

5. Low-fat diets are dramatically low in vitamins A, D, E, F and K— the very nutrients you need to maintain a healthy heart and circulatory system. Conversely, low-fat diets lack the fat necessary for your body to absorb many of the nutrients from fruits and vegetables.

6. Almost no one can persist on a diet of 20 percent fat. Depression sets in, life becomes a bore and social well-being is distorted. The Mediterranean diet (see Appendix) is a better diet. It offers better health, is delicious and is easy to stick with.

7. The Zone diet, Sugar Busters, Atkins, Ornish, Pritiken and the rest all have something to offer. But the research shows that it is a *simple* reduction **in calories** that causes you to lose weight. While insulin is critical, the simplistic reasoning for the relationship between insulin and their diets is flawed. In fact, the Mediterranean diet is better than all of these.

8. All the low fat, zero-cholesterol concoctions are un-healthy products loaded with **trans fats**. Prefabricated meals and snacks from ConAgra ("food factories") and others are a disaster for your heart and health. The

olive oil-rich Mediterranean diet contains no trans fats at all.

9. An olive oil Mediterranean diet as consumed in Crete and Spain, is even healthier than a Japanese diet. Japanese people consuming a lower-fat diet had much more heart disease than did Cretans consuming higher fat and a Mediterranean fare. While the Japanese diet has benefits over the average American diet, it is definitely not the best. In fact, the Japanese suffer from large numbers of strokes (probably due to the low fat intake and low cholesterol levels) and high rates of cancer.

10. **Spain, the largest producer of olive oil, has the greatest life expectancy in the Western world.**

11. Extreme low-fat diets of 20 percent fat—while disastrous to your health—are considered very healthy by most American physicians

12. Eighty-two percent of polled physicians had no idea that low-fat diets *lower HDL* (high density lipid, the good fat) levels in the body.

Liquid Candy

Everything about soft drinks is BIG—big ad budgets, big sales, big serving sizes. They're a big part of our diets and a big health problem. And there's good reason to believe that the popularity of soft drinks will increase. "This year, even as we sell one billion servings of our products daily, the world will still consume 47 billion servings of other beverages everyday," say Coca-Cola's 1997 annual report. "We're just getting started."

In 1997, Americans spent more than $54 billion on soft drinks. **Every drop was a missed opportunity to drink water, nature's cleansing drink. Instead, we're drowning in *liquid candy*.**

In 1997, Americans spent more than $54 billion on soft drinks... we're drowning in *liquid candy*.

Big Ad Budgets

In 1997, Coca-Cola spent $277 million to advertise its sodas. Pepsi spent close to $200 million. The National Cancer Institute spends less than $1 million a year on its 5-A-Day program (five servings of fruits and vegetables), which encourages people to eat more fruits and vegetables.

What Americans Drink

Americans drank twice as many soft drinks in 1997 as they did in 1973 and 43 percent more than in 1985. We gulp six times more soda than fruit juice. Manufacturers pump out enough soda pop to give every American 54 gallons a year—that's 19 ounces a day. The average teenage boy downs 3 1/2 cans (42 oz.) of soda a day; one in ten drinks seven cans a day. Girls average three-quarters as much soda as boys.

It's Everywhere

"We're putting ice-cold Coca-Cola classic and our other brands within reach, wherever you look: at the supermarket, the video store, the soccer field, the gas station—everywhere," says Coca-Cola's 1997 annual report. More than 2.8 million vending machines spew out more than 27 billion soft drinks a year.

Kidney Stones

In men who previously had kidney stones, those who refrained from drinking sodas that contained phosphoric acid were less likely to get new stones. Phosphoric acid is found in colas. Check the label.

Big Servings

Soda serving sizes have grown from a 6 1/2-ounce bottle in the 1950's to 20-ounce bottles today. At fast food restaurants, a "child"-size soft drink is 12 ounces and a "small" is 16 ounces. At 7-11 convenience stores, the Double Gulp is 64 ounces.

Big Calories

A 12-ounce can of a non-diet cola has about 10 teaspoons of sugar and 150 calories. A large Coke at fast food restaurants (32-ounces with ice) has 310 calories. The previously-mentioned "Double Gulp" could have twice that much. Overweight teens get a larger percentage of their calories from soft drinks than do other teens. While this is not proof that soda causes *obesity*, it is worrisome.

Going After Kids

Colorado Springs School District II will receive between $8 million and $11 million over the next ten years from its exclusive contract to sell Coca-Cola products in its vending machines.

Big Buzz

Caffeine is a mildly addictive stimulant drug that's added to most cola and "pepper" drinks and some other sodas. The average male teenage soda drinker downs enough caffeine to equal 1 1/2 cups of coffee a day.

You Must Stick With It!

The patient with the worst problem we encountered on the Pilot Program was Bryan (name changed). A patient of mine suggested that Bryan be a part of the program. He or his parents had taken him to all the famous clinics without lasting success. I left it up to the parents to decide if they wanted to be a part of the study. After interviewing everyone in the family, we knew Bryan wanted to be better. He was home schooled because he couldn't get along with other children at the school he had attended. I am glad he did not quit. When we met him, Bryan had been taking up to twenty-one prescription medications a day after being diagnosed by his medical physician. The diagnosis was given after five to six hours of testing. He had been under a physicians care for eight years and was sixteen when we met. His diagnosis included ADHD, dysthymic depression disorder, allergies, asthma and "chicken skin." His symptoms without medication included being distractive, impulsive, difficulty in doing work and regular bouts of pneumonia and bronchitis. Needless to say, he was not happy. Bryan was determined to get better.

They understood that we were his last hope. He did not have it easy. He had much anger and was not safe to be around. Because of his "anger," he actually opened the door of a car that was moving. He bent silverware at the table because of the same "anger." Bryan was still having mood swings and anger through the seventy-fourth day in the program. He had no antibiotics for three months. This was the first time in his life he was able to go that long without them. Days eighty-four and eighty-five were the best he had been in his life. He was happy and having fun. His mother really helped support him through the process. He followed the protocol like the other participants. We did spinal correction on him and he also completed several colon cleanses with a colon therapist.

A real thrill for him was the snow skiing he was able to do for the first time in his life without getting sick. Bryan was also very pleased that his skin condition ("chicken skin") had completely cleared up. He had been told that he would live with that forever. Bryan lost weight on the program, losing twenty-eight pounds in ninety days. One year later after he completed the program, he was able to go on a missions trip to Asia for one month which he paid for by himself by working odd jobs for people at his church. Bryan is now consistently happy, aware of his diet, continuing with spinal alignment and natural supplementation choices.

Steps to Optimum Health

**This needs to be an entire family cooperative!
Everyone benefits in a positive way with
his or her own improvement!**

Below is one week of a lunch menu utilized by a Ritalin user of several years. This is a standard menu that has hidden hydrogenated fat, sugar and dairy products which precipitates an imbalance in the masses of children in our society today. This particular menu comes from a private school; the public school sector contains even more refined carbohydrates, dairy and hydrogenated fats. These foods are not fresh and come from processed commercial sources.

LUNCH MENU for Grades K - 5 and 6 -12				
Available every day: Salad and Peanut Butter/Jelly Sandwich				
MONDAY	**TUESDAY**	**WEDNESDAY**	**THURSDAY**	**FRIDAY**
25	**26**	**27**	**28**	**29**
Pizza	Chickenburger	Hot Dog	Lasagna	
Salad or Applesauce	Lettuce & Tomato	Spudsters	Breadstick	
	Potato Wedges			
Peaches		Carrots & Celery	Salad or Applesauce	
	Mixed Fruit			
		Jell-O	Carrots	
Choc. Cup Cake				
	Toffee Cookie			
Milk		Assorted Cookies	Vanilla Pudding	TBA
	Milk		Milk	CLASS LUNCH $2
		Milk		

The information provided to us by the National School Lunch Program causes confusion. We are told that fats, oils and sweets should be the smallest part of the American Food Pyramid because they provide high calories and low nutrition. I agree. However, we are not taught the difference between what foods are truly good for us and what foods may, in fact, be toxic. A part of that challenge is the fact that health care providers and the parties involved don't always agree. **The thought of chemically-modified cow's milk being a negative factor is a revolutionary thought for most in our society today.**

An ideal lunch would consist of no hydrogenated fats, minimal or no dairy and, most importantly, no sugar. What chance does a child have by consuming cookies, pudding and a drink loaded with sugar? I have found the best results are achieved by preparing your own meals, including packing food for times when you are out of the home.

An ideal lunch would consist of no hydrogenated fats, minimal or no dairy and, most importantly, no sugar.

Slowly incorporate foods without sugar and hydrogenated fats. Read labels. Locate a food co-op in your area that has "health food." We use the Forc Co-op; call 1.888.936.9648 for information on one in your area.

I have enclosed a copy of a typical national school lunch program. We are told that fat should be a small part of the pyramid, but dairy proves to be the exception. Milk is served daily for breakfast and lunch. By reviewing the food choices that these children are given, it becomes quite obvious that if the child consumes these foods for breakfast and lunch, they are going to consume an abundance of ingredients that are now known to cause major health problems, including hyperactivity.

Elementary Breakfast & Lunch Menu

MONDAY	TUESDAY	WEDNESDAY	THURSDAY	FRIDAY
9	10	11	12	13
Chocolate Honey Bun	Fruit Danish	Danimal Yogurt w/Fruit	Apple Streusel	Fruit Pop Tart
Apple Juice	Pineapple Juice	Strawberry Waffle	Cheese Stick	Applesauce
Milk	Milk	Milk	Milk	Milk
Pizza Burrito	Grand Slam	Hamburger w/Bun	Pizza	Pizza
Garden Salad	Chicken Nuggets	Ketchup, Mustarad, Pickle Slices	Veggie Pasta Salad	Green Beans
Diced Pears	Bread Stick, Tator Tots	Veggie Crunchies w/Dip	Cherry Applesauce	Fluffy Rice Dessert w/Fruit
Milk	Raspberry Sherbert	Fresh Banana	Milk	Milk
	Milk	Milk		

My research shows that dairy products can lead to various sensitivities in individuals, compounded by the fact that every day, some type of hydrogenated fat ingredients are in their breakfast food. These children are fed food that is causing an imbalance. Some school programs feel milk is so essential that a note is required for kids not to drink milk.

It has been recently reported by Congress, that the "school lunches are still inadequate." The fat content goal has not been met.

A patient of mine, a local school bus driver, pointed out that 90 percent of foods provided to school children today are pre-made. Children start the day with poor quality breakfasts foods either at school, at home or on the run to school. She asked the students on her bus route what they ate for breakfast. I have included a list of these foods from 200 school children surveyed.

Number of Children	What they ate for breakfast	Number of Children	What they ate for breakfast
37	Nothing	2	Candy
89	Cereal	2	Chocolate chip cookies
35	Toast/Bagels	25	Milk/Chocolate Milk
16	Pancakes/Waffles	3	Coffee
2	Bacon	2	Pepsi
1	Oatmeal	2	Fruit
8	Pop Tarts	11	Fruit Juice

Children often do not get enough food at child care centers to obtain even 50 percent of the RDA for energy, niacin, iron and zinc.

My son David was diagnosed with ADHD and SID (sensory integration dysfunction) this past spring. I took him to a behavioral pediatrician who recommended Ritalin for him. Although I wasn't very comfortable with medicating David, I went along with it because David was struggling so much in school and a lot at home too due to his lack of impulse control mainly. He also had a lot of trouble going to sleep at night because he was so wound up. The medication did help him a little but it sure wasn't worth the nose-dive his appetite suffered as a side effect. David is a thin child. We tried a different medication to see if that would be better and it was until we added a second medication.

About the time we started the second medication, I consulted Dr. Bob. He recommended dietary changes. The behavioral pediatrician had told me that dietary changes were not proven to be effective in treating ADHD. By the middle of July, I had David's diet free of dairy, hydrogenated fats and refined sugar. I also started giving him vitamins and mineral supplements. The first change I noticed was his problems falling asleep significantly improved. The last week of July, first of August I sent him to my parents for a visit. They could tell that he was a lot calmer. He started Kindergarten at the end of August (with an aide). I was concerned with all the stimulation he might still need medication. Although he still has his days where he doesn't focus all that well on his assignments, he is doing better than I ever thought he would after the problems he had in preschool last year.

It was really difficult changing David's diet so that he has things he likes to eat but I am so glad I did. Even if your child likes ice cream like David, there are substitute products that taste good! Rice Dream makes something that is like a Klondike bar that David loves. He wasn't too happy about eating plain Rice Dream until I found the Oh Fudge topping that Wax Orchards makes. There are a lot of products out there that do not taste very good so it was a lot of trial and error. It seems really overwhelming, but it is really worth the trouble.

I am so thankful that I consulted Dr. Bob. I had been praying for God to direct me to the right treatment for David and he did!

Annette, David's Mom

> Drinking five glasses of water daily,
> decreases the risk of colon cancer by 45 percent,
> plus it can slash the risk of breast cancer
> by 79 percent, and one is 50 percent less likely
> to develop bladder cancer.

NOTES

10

The Transition

The Plan

There has been an ongoing debate on how to treat hyperactivity, ADD, ADHD, ODD. Parents may fear altering their child's medication, fear that the child may be removed from school, fear poor grades will result, fear that their doctor may be upset, etc. Medical doctors and natural practitioners are trained to take a history, complete an exam, run tests and prescribe a plan of treatment. Medical physicians unlike natural-holistic practitioners are programmed by training, peer pressure, pharmaceutical companies, patients and economic gain to prescribe drugs. Suggesting any other option to a medical doctor is inviting a battle. They are not trained to "think" naturally or holistically. For most traditionally-trained health care providers, dietary modifications are unrelated to hyperactivity, just as they believe diet does not affect skin challenges, digestion, etc., etc.

Natural health care providers seek natural treatment programs. You will need to "shop around" your area until you find someone who will listen. Ask your local health food store owner or manager. They normally know which health care providers use natural, back-to-basic remedies.

The basic transition to healthfulness from Hyperactivity, ADD, ADHD, ODD is the following:

☑ **Eliminate hydrogenated fats. Cleanse Your Body!**

Eliminate trans fats from the diet for a minimum of 102 days (pre-packaged foods, french fries, snack foods including chips, cookies, etc.). **You need to use the three-month plus time period because it takes approximately 102 days to better health and cleanse the toxins from your system.**

Do not expect an overnight miracle by changing your diet. There are alternatives to common foods without hydrogenated fats. You will need to utilize the health food section in your grocery store, health food store or order products on-line. I strongly recommend you begin making your foods from scratch.

Remember, hydrogenated fats are altered chemical structures that interfere with the metabolism of fats in your body, which is the number one reason why you and/or your family has challenges and problems with hyperactivity.

☑ Eliminate dairy products for minimum of 102 days

Dairy products need to be avoided for a minimum of 102 days. The fatty acid in the milk or dairy product, when out of balance and over consumed, interferes with the metabolism of the pain-relieving fats in your body. An example is that people start their day with milk on their cereal. *Elimination of all dairy products for a minimum of 102 days is essential.* Know that this will be a major challenge for school systems, moms, dads and health care providers. I'm not saying that eventually you can't go back to small amounts of dairy, but we need to give your body a chance to normalize fat metabolism. Chocolate milk is not safe and something your child should never consume.

☑ Eliminate all refined sugar

Eliminate, if possible, corn syrup, fruit juices, dried fruits, and very sweet fruits (bananas, grapes, raisins, pineapple). I have found that these fruits help raise insulin levels. Raising insulin levels leads to increased sugar cravings (Eat pears, plums, apples; also, see Star Sweeteners).

☑ Discontinue eating foods containing additives, preservatives, and artificial flavorings and colorings

These foods can interfere with fat metabolism in the body. This is a trigger for some children. I prefer as a priority the elimination of hydrogenated fats. There has not been consistency with the preservative, additive theory.

☑ Determine allergic foods and eliminate them from the diet

There are foods that can directly enter the blood stream, especially if there is inadequate anti-inflammatory oil, which builds proper tissues in the body, e.g., flax oil. These food particles can abruptly go through the intestinal system and wreak havoc on your immune system. I encourage patients to avoid foods that they crave. You can make this decision by utilizing the Elimination Diet (see Appendix). In time, you may go back to some foods to which you may currently appear to be sensitive. By eliminating foods that are causing a negative reaction in your body, you are giving your body a chance to be in a normal state of health.

☑ Supplement Protocol is on pages 121 and 150.

Utilizing the vitamins and minerals I am suggesting will aid in your child's improved health. Ingesting vitamin Bs and minerals will restore balance with the body.

☑ Subluxation Check Up in Chapter 16.

Good, Better, Best
Never Let It Rest
Until Good Becomes Better
And Better Becomes Rest

The following is an excellent transitional chart for making a smooth transition to healthier foods. This information was taken in part from, *Junk Food to Real Food, A Blueprint for Healthier Eating*, by Carol A. Nostrand.

Transition Chart

Food to Avoid PROTEINS	Food to Enjoy PROTEINS	
Eliminate Immediately	***Acceptable Foods*** *Experiment with These*	***Vital Foods*** *Primarily Use These*
Meats with additives, such as luncheon meat packed with nitrites (bologna, salami, etc.)	Meat without additives, hormones, antibiotics, etc., raised free-range on organic feed	Sprouts Fresh, raw nuts and seeds: flax, chia, pumpkin, sunflower, sesame, almond, pecan, brazil, walnut, filbert, etc.
Meat with hormones, etc.	Deep ocean or pure-lake fish	
Processed cheese		
Processed eggs	Nuts and grain as the source to make rice, almond milk, cheese, and yogurt	Nut butters
Processed chicken– *raised in small coops, injected with antibiotics,* etc.		Nut milks Organic eggs
	Goat's milk, chevre, feta cheese (Goat's milk is very close to human milk constituents) and is acceptable, but not daily.	Beans: lentils, split peas, black beans, etc.
Pork		
Pasteurized, homogenized cow's milk		Tofu, tempeh
Yogurt with sugar, and toxic additives		

Food to Avoid **CARBOHYDRATES**	Food to Enjoy **CARBOHYDRATES**	
Eliminate Immediately	*Acceptable Foods* *Experiment with These*	*Vital Foods* *Primarily Use These*
Sugar: white, brown, turbinado, sucrose, glucose, corn syrup, fructose, etc.	Raw honey; blackstrap molasses; barley malt; pure maple syrup	Vegetables: squash, carrots, celery, tomatoes, beets, cabbage, broccoli, cauliflower, leeks, turnips, radish, lettuce, etc.
Chocolate	Carob	
Processed carbohydrates such as white flour and white flour products	Whole grain bread	Fruit: apple, pears, plums, apples, etc.
White rice	Whole grain pasta	Sea vegetables
Anything packaged or canned with sugar, salt or toxic additives	Grain/Nut ice cream made without toxic additives or sugar	Whole grains: brown rice, millet, rye, barley, etc.
Processed pasta		
Ice cream with sugar and toxic additives		

Food to Avoid **LIPIDS**	Food to Enjoy **LIPIDS**	
Eliminate Immediately	*Acceptable Foods* *Experiment with These*	*Vital Foods* *Primarily Use These*
Oils that are rancid or overheated	High Oleic safflower, sunflower, olive oil	Raw, cold-processed oils: olive, sunflower, sesame, flax, almond, walnut, avocado
Rancid animal fats, such as lard, bacon drippings, etc.	Butter	Raw, unsalted butter
Anything deep-fat fried		Avocado
Artificially hardened fats, such as margarine and shortenings		Fresh, raw nuts and seeds

Food to Avoid OTHER		Food to Enjoy OTHER
Eliminate Immediately	*Acceptable Foods* *Experiment with These*	*Vital Foods* *Primarily Use These*
Coffee, tannic-acid teas; excess alcohol	Pure grain coffee substitutes	Herb teas and seasonings
Common table salt (sodium chloride)	Not more than one glass a day of non-chemicalized wine or beer	Organic apple cider vinegar
Any commercial condiments with sugar, salt or toxic additives	Aluminum-free baking powder	Home-made condiments without salt or sugar
Commercial soft drinks made with toxic additives and sugar	Soft drinks made without chemicals, sugar or toxic additives	Freshly juiced vegetables and fruits
	Potassium balanced salt; celtic sea salt	Fresh fruit ice cream
	Vegetable salt and kelp	Reverse osmosis purified water

Calcium Substitute

The milk mustache advertising campaign is physiologically misleading. Milk has a solid reputation of being a healthy and essential product. How milk influences the body is very complicated, although the American Dairy Association would have you believe otherwise.

Flavored milk products are now finding their way into school vending machines. Is this a healthy alternative? Absolutely not! Flavored milk has more calories and as much sugar as soda and contains 460 calories. With the decreased sales of milk, this is just another marketing scheme to get milk to a large portion of the soda-consuming population. School kids are offered the two beverage options (soda and milk) that contribute to their lower state of health. Again, is it about a health-conscious milk industry or a money-hungry milk industry?

Health care providers and people who understand human physiology are aware that a majority of the world does not drink or consume cow's milk and dairy products. This issue must be addressed because there will be those who insist that humans need milk.

According to the American Dairy Association, it is a "no brainer" that milk is necessary for proper bone health. Animal protein (yes, milk is a protein) is an acid and requires calcium to be balanced, therefore dairy consumption leads to calcium loss.

In my health-centered practice, I promote minimal or no milk consumption. I do not have cow's milk in my home. My sons do not have cavities, migrating joint pain, acne, asthma or hyperactivity. Milk consumption leads to migrating pain, sinus problems and a huge list of unhealthful conditions, including ear infections.

Medical practitioners either do not understand, or simply do not know, that milk causes ear infections. Do your own research. Eliminate milk (white and chocolate) from your child's diet, substitute with rice, almond or other nut milks for breakfast cereal. Supplement their diet with sesame seeds, almonds or calcium citrate and increase water consumption. I guarantee you will notice a reduction in childhood "sickness," especially ear infections.

When eliminating calcium, some may be concerned about osteoporosis. I encourage minimal sugar consumption because sugar depletes calcium. I tell our patients to eat almonds (while I have not seen sensitivities with almonds, I do see major correlations between peanut consumption and poor health), which are a neutral nut and a good source of fat (I know you may be concerned about fat, but this is a healthy fat.) Sesame seeds and Romaine lettuce are a good source of calcium. Spinach has phytic acid that depletes calcium. Broccoli, cabbage and cauliflower are cruciferous foods, and a good source of calcium (but have been shown to suppress thyroid function and effecting calcium metabolism).

If you or your family has a history of dental breakdown, evaluate your eating habits (which inevitably you pass to your children). It is not to say you can never drink milk again but, instead, limit your consumption until you evaluate the results of dairy removal. Try to get your calcium from other calcium-rich foods (i.e., almonds), not from calcium carbonate found in "digestive aids." I discourage fortified juices with added calcium. Concentrated juices are heated and are poor sources of living nutrients and enzymes. Create your own juice daily with a mix of your favorite vegetables.

COMPARISON: ALMOND vs. MILK (3½ oz.)				
NUTRIENT	ALMOND Raw Unsalted	COW'S MILK 3.5% fat	COW'S MILK 3.7% fat	SKIM MILK
CALCIUM	234mg	188mg	117mg	121mg

Almonds, raw and unsalted, contain twice as much calcium as the same quantity of milk. Almonds are an excellent way of getting high quality calcium without using dairy products.

I have not suggested soy as a viable substitute for dairy. My current research reveals that soy may be an over-processed, hard to digest anti-nutrient. I limit my patient's recommended level of soy consumption to 8 ounces daily.

Today, nearly half of all U.S. adults say they take vitamins, and one out of four use herbal supplements.

11

Hype-Free Food

Breakfast Suggestions

Breakfast can come from any source other than from a package, a can, an envelope, a powder, etc. Rotating foods is important. Breakfast will affect insulin levels in your child, which makes a major impact on the craving for sugar. Avoid starting the day with sweets, syrups and packaged foods. Sugar cravings are not only a sign of a mineral need but also of an improper functioning body. Where should you start?

Avoid bananas, dates, figs, grapes and raisins in the morning. These foods will raise insulin and cause blood sugar variations and can effect the production of prostaglandins. Use wholesome non-sugar breakfast cereals with soymilk, rice milk or almond milk. Soy yogurt is excellent on cereal, but some do contain evaporated cane juice. Bake a coconut. (Drill holes to let milk out, cook 325 for 10 minutes—mmmmmm, good!) Don't limit yourself to traditional breakfast choices.

☑ **Oatmeal** is a simple food. It takes less than seven minutes. Boiling water, adding oats and letting it simmer for five minutes, sprinkled with Celtic Sea Salt and possibly some added applesauce (which has been homemade by you). Remember, almonds and sesame seeds are a great source of calcium; walnuts and pecans are an excellent source of Omega 3 oils; pumpkin seeds, sunflower seeds and any other seeds that you can think of can be put into the oatmeal. Add anything that you know your child may enjoy.

☑ **Rice cakes** with almond butter, sesame butter or cashew butter spread on them. Add a dash of real fruit jelly (one teaspoon). Avoid commercially prepared jelly (from nationally known chains) containing fructose, corn syrup or sucrose. Use no-sugar added jellies.

☑ **Multi-grain pancakes** made with water, soymilk or rice milk. Spread jelly containing no sugar. My sons make their own pancakes with natural Pancake and Waffle Mix. We add soymilk for the liquid. Applesauce on pancakes with cinnamon is tasty. Real maple syrup can be used—not "fake" syrup. (This is a good Saturday breakfast enabling you to monitor your child's blood sugar results).

☑ **Breakfast cereals.** Health food stores contain many varieties. Read the ingredients. Look for cereals that do not contain corn syrup or hydrogenated fats. Remember, we need to avoid hydrogenated fats. No sugar coated cereals including, corn, wheat or rice products.

☑ **Eggs** are an excellent source of protein and sulfur that is important for the production of collagen in the body. Scrambled, poached or fried with butter.

☑ **Whole wheat bread** is definitely better than white bread. Your child may have problems with wheat, which may be due to the lack of fat that is needed to process wheat. Gluten may also be an issue with some individuals. We have found Ezekiel Bread, which is a sprouted grain bread to be an excellent substitute for white bread, which I normally refer to as styrofoam bread. Spelt grain is an ancient grain that will put less stress on your child's digestive process. There is also millet, rice bread and nut breads. Go to your freezer section at your local health food store and/or check out any number of the sources I have included for gluten-free bread. Make your own bread.

☑ **Minimal or no dairy.** *Dairy can alter the production of the Omega 3 fat.* A part of the challenge that we have today is that we consume too much dairy. The dairy business believes we need more dairy products; we still consume macaroni and cheese, pizza, yogurt and ice cream. I was raised on cow's milk and did not have a problem with hyperactivity. However, I did not drink milk exclusively, and it was not laced with hormones as it is today. I also am aware that not all children will have a hyperactive reaction to milk. I also know that consuming dairy products can result in chronic ear infections resulting in antibiotic prescriptions. This is also why I encourage people not to consume dairy.

☑ **No pork.** Pork is not the other white meat. Pork is toxic. Whatever the pig eats, you eat. Pigs wallow in their own fecal material and eat anything.

☑ **Yogurt.** You can use soy yogurt. Add sesame seeds, almonds, flax seeds, a sprinkle of raisins, all are an excellent source of protein. Unfortunately, it is now difficult to find soy yogurt without evaporated cane juice crystals, this may cause a problem with continued sugar craving.

☑ **Cheese.** I would encourage you to use rice cheese or soy cheese. There are individually sliced sheets of rice cheese with American cheese flavor for toasted cheese sandwiches. There is also mozzarella individually sliced cheese that can be used to make a variety of foods. Goat cheese! Feta and chevre. We use Chevre in our home. Goat's milk is the closest to human milk. We put our Chevre in a manually locked container with a rubber gasket ring and let it set in infused olive oil. Infused olive oil means that we take good quality virgin olive oil and put sun dried tomatoes, basil, parsley, thyme, chives and oregano and let those herbs soak in the oil for about three weeks then pour it off. Infused oil can be used as an excellent base for your cooking needs.

☑ **Squash.** Bake or fry squash, season it with cinnamon. If you present this in a very loving way and you yourself eat the squash, I guarantee your children will eat the squash also.

☑ **Juice.** I encourage patients not to consume orange juice or grapefruit juice especially when the temperature goes below 60 degrees(mucus congestion will occur in the intestines when the outside temp is 60 degrees or lower (as stated by my colonic therapist). Minimize oranges and grapefruits; they appear to cause pain in patients. People have citrus sensitivities usually due to a deficiency of panthothenic acid. Apple cider and apple juice are good alternatives. Vary the juices.

☑ **Water.** No tap water. The average glass of tap water has been through six toilets. Use reverse osmosis or spring water. Vary your spring water sources; some may not be any better than tap water.

☑ **Meat.** Organic meat is best. Organic ground beef, turkey, chicken or lamb can be used in a variety of ways. Use some imagination.

Lunch Suggestions

Packing lunches is an important part of the program. Remind your child not to swap lunches because this could precipitate their hyperactivity, ADHD, ADD or ODD. What can you pack for lunch? First, you may want to purchase a cooler pack containing "blue ice." My sons have packed their own lunches since they were in third grade. You need to supervise. Let them make choices, but provide a variety of ideas and the "fixins."

NOTICE
I believe that the school lunch program in America is precipitating our hyperactivity problem. Commonly filled with high sugar, dairy and hydrogenated fats.

We get antibiotic- nitrate-free turkey from the health food store. You can make almond butter and jelly sandwiches. Vary the bread and jelly. You can use pita bread, flat bread and any grain, but vary it. Veggie salads, tuna salad, egg salad, turkey salad, chicken salad sandwiches with rice cheese, lettuce and safflower mayo or whatever condiment you prefer. Soy cheese pizza, pizza bagels, almond butter on celery and other fresh cut up veggies. Make whole pasta with butter or soymilk in a container that keeps the contents warm. **You must read all labels.**

I have included a sample letter requesting that your child not be given milk (see Chapter 17). You or your health care provider can sign this letter.

You can use soy yogurt, tofu meat products and carob rice cakes.

No peanuts. Yeast and mold symptoms will appear with daily peanut consumption. Peanut butter is a common food consumed by patients with behavior challenges. This precipitates the need for antibiotics and a continued immune system beak down.

No hydrogenated-fat chips. There are chips made with safflower oil or olive oil.

No french fries cooked with hydrogenated fats.

Condiments containing no sugar or corn syrup are best purchased from a health food store. Most condiments today, including the major commercial brands, always seem to contain sugar.

Dinner Suggestions

Not having your child on medication alone should justify the additional time spent on food preparation. Dinner is a very interesting meal. Families rarely unite at the kitchen table for

It is estimated that more than one-half of meals are eaten out of the home, including dinner.

dinner as they have in the past. It is estimated that more than one-half of meals are eaten out of the home, including dinner.

You are going to have a family meeting to make decisions as to what type of food you would like to be preparing for your evening meals. Make it a fun, cooperative event where everyone participates, creating a unit for discussion and laughter.

You can eat anything you want *except* pork, hydrogenated fats, pre-packaged/powdered/boxed or canned food that contains preservatives and/or artificial colorings, flavorings, etc. We do eat meat (normally organic, antibiotic-free), but you do not have to have red meat with every meal. We utilize pastas, beans, legumes and a variety of casseroles.

I encourage you to purchase as much food as you can fresh, therefore after you are finished with a meal, instead of having it as a leftover you could freeze it and have it at another time. I encourage individuals to pre-bake several meals prior to the beginning of the week. There are an enormous variety of foods that can be used, i.e., squashes, zucchini, eggplant, potatoes, yams as well as a variety of casseroles. In other words—make your food from scratch!

Your ethnic background and food taste will determine the type of foods you like to eat. Your goal is fresh, organic and alive food. Varying foods is important. In our household we use different organic tomato-based sauces, organic starter-type foods (organic broths).

You don't need to use or consume dessert. I'm not exactly sure where this habit started, however, ending a meal with sugar puts enormous stress on the liver, pancreas, and digestive system. Your body is busy breaking down simple carbohydrates and adding proteins to it can confuse the body. Utilizing and putting sugar on top of this causes an enormous overload on the pancreas.

I have included several recipes that you can use to get started. You could find some of Grandma's old recipes and use them, but be cautious of the amount of sugar.

BE CREATIVE! Canned and pre-packaged food are often mineral depleting, metabolism altering, toxin creating chemical time bombs.

Salmon, tuna, eggs and chicken can all be used. There is even turkey bacon, turkey sausage and lamb sausage. Fake bacon, fake chicken—tofu alternatives, but remember to read labels because some of those products contain unhealthy oils, sugar and preservatives.

I would encourage you to visit a bookstore, health food store and even the Internet for favorite recipes that you can utilize. There are many wonderful health magazines that have numerous recipes.

Sweet Suggestions

I have included several recipes that you can use—homemade, of course—but there are other sources of naturally made cookies and desserts that can be purchased at your local health food store.

Amaranth is an ancient flour product that can be used in replacement of wheat. There are nut and grain ice creams. We have rave results every time we take apple crisp with ice cream to somebody's house.

Snacks

I encourage patients to consume a minimum of one apple, one carrot and a quart of water per day along with their other normal food choices. Having wholesome homemade snacks is ideal. By utilizing a food co-op, you can often purchase very good snacks that are made with the proper ingredients.

Keep cut-up vegetables and fruits on hand for yourself and family. *Consume fruits only on an empty stomach*, not after a meal.

Vary your snacks. There are healthy snack foods available without hydrogenated fats including cookies without sugar. Popcorn made with olive oil or an air popper is excellent.

Visit health food stores, look into a food co-op. You can find excellent baking mixes having very simple ingredients. Have your children bake with you. This is a great wintertime activity. My sons participate in school activities and other sports, but they love to get their hands in dough.

If you Insist on Frying or Deep Frying

Heating oils and hydrogenated fat is a leading cause of hyperactivity.

Frying and deep frying are two of the most popular methods of (fast) food preparation. And they are the two most damaging to health. Heating oils and hydrogenated fat is a leading cause of hyperactivity. Light, air and heat cause chemical changes in oils.

Frying and deep-frying result in rapid oxidation as well as other chemical changes that occur in oils that are subjected to high temperature in the presence of light and oxygen. For example, free radicals are produced, a known contributor to health problems.

Frying with oil seems harmless in the short term, but over time, our cells accumulate these toxins. There is no such thing as "safe" frying; frying temperatures are too high. When food turns brown, it literally has been burned. When consumed, fried food will affect fat metabolism.

There are some oils in which heat reduces the negative impact. One should never heat oil with high essential fatty acids: flax, primrose, rose and borage or black currant oils. Although frying in general is not recommended for health, some oils and some frying methods are better than others.

These can be helpful for those who do not want to give up this destructive practice.

Wok cooking with oil has become quite popular. Traditional Chinese cooks first put water in the wok. Water keeps the temperature down. Putting food in the pan first, then adding the oil, results in food tasting less burned. More natural flavors are preserved. Remember, if you insist on frying/deep frying, the less oils are heated, the better.

Frying and deep-frying destroys all oil and cannot be recommended for health. However, if your child insists on consuming fried foods, I have included a list of options. You will need to cook at home. Although they are attempting to change, fast food restaurants currently do not have "healthy fries." These restaurants are not going away, and we need for them to provide healthier options.

Frying destroys some oils more than others. If you must fry, use refined oils that contain the lowest amount of essential fatty acids and the greatest amount of saturated fats (butter) and monosaturated fats (olive oil). Garlic and onions are high sulfur foods and minimize free radical damage.

> **If you must fry, use refined oils that contain the lowest amount of essential fatty acids and the greatest amount of saturated fats (butter) and monosaturated fats (olive oil).**

Oils least damaged by high temperatures and oxygen include:

- ☑ Butter
- ☑ GHEE (sourced from butter)
- ☑ Tropical fats (coconut)
- ☑ High oleic sunflower
- ☑ High oleic safflower
- ☑ Peanut oil
- ☑ Sesame oil
- ☑ Olive oil

Frying/deep-frying is not going to lead to optimal health. Yet, sometimes the alternative that does less harm is better than continuing with more toxic methods.

COST OF FOOD

Eating healthier will drastically reduce money spent stocking our medicine cabinets.

Consider your cost of over-the-counter medications—antacids, sinus medications and pain killers—to treat symptoms of improper eating. Eating healthier will drastically reduce money spent stocking your medicine cabinets.

I often hear individuals complain that it is expensive to eat healthy. Many health food stores today have competitive prices. The cost for organic food may be slightly higher than commercially prepared food due to supply and demand. My wife and I strategically shop after the middle of the month. We have a chest freezer. Prices in health food stores, from my experience, usually are lower in the second part of the month. They have sales correlative to pay periods and third party assistance (Social Security). Attempt to buy food on sale. "European" grocery stores carry wonderful and healthy foods at a price far lower than health food stores. Utilize a food co-op. You can save hundreds of dollars every month. Find local food producers. During harvest time, you can freeze many of the foods. Living healthy requires some work and participation. Plan out meals.

Compare how much money you spend every time you eat out versus making that same food at home. Although it takes time, remember we need to spend more time with each other than we have in the past.

12

Hype-Free Sassy Sweeteners

Your Guide to Understanding Sweeteners

Most of my patients have questions about sugar and natural sugar alternatives. Increased sugar consumption is a contributing factor to behavioral challenges, and it is a leading cause of many other health conditions as well. Because you might have chronic sinusitis, migraines, headaches or back pain, it is very important for you to understand why you need to be a label reader.

The average American consumes 149 pounds of refined sugar each year. If your body were to convert this, it would add 79 pounds of fat. By calculating the amount of sugar that comes from soda consumption, it is easy to see why our children are in a diminished state of health. Most Americans eat too much refined sugar, which travels through your mouth and stomach tissues right to your bloodstream. This wreaks havoc on your blood sugar levels and your immune system.

Our human instinct to seek sweeteners is so strong that an unborn baby will make swallowing motions when its mother is injected with a sweetener. Our intense instinct for sweeteners causes us to seek out sweet breast milk. Even in adulthood, sugar continues to be a common craving. How many of you had

---

something sweet to eat within the last 24-48 hours? If not, do you plan on having something sweet very shortly?

Sweet, appealing foods have become hopelessly intertwined with pleasure and euphoria. These foods are alluring, symbolizing reward or comfort. After a hard day at work or school, devouring a candy bar seems to be a valid reward (or a survival mechanism). Sugar causes our brains to release endorphins, a "feel good" chemical. Yet, it is not white sugar or derivatives that your body wants—it wants complex carbohydrates that are as whole as mother's milk.

All sugars are not created equal. Some would say there is no differentiation between natural or refined sugars because our bodies use both for energy. Sugars can be either simple or complex carbohydrates. Natural sugars are almost always complex carbohydrates; white (or refined) sugars are almost always simple carbohydrates. Complex carbohydrates (like those in beans, fruit, vegetables and whole grains) are made of long chains of simple sugar. Your body digests them more slowly and provides your blood with a more balanced sugar supply. Whatever sugar your body doesn't immediately need is stored in your liver as glycogen, an energy reserve for a rainy day.

You cannot have fat breakdown or fat metabolism with elevated insulin levels.

White sugar is a human invention, not a gift from nature. In 1795, Louisiana farmers devised a cheaper way to granulate sugar on a large scale, which made white sugar available to the masses.

Complex carbohydrates give you all the energy you need. When you are looking for something to satisfy your sweet tooth, however, turn to natural sweeteners like rice and barley malt syrups that are 50 percent complex carbohydrates. Our body's digestive enzymes break these two types of sugars down to glucose, a sugar that the body uses for energy.

The difference between simple and complex carbohydrates is how quickly each enters the blood stream and how each affects insulin in blood sugar levels, a real key to the reason I believe we have major problems with obesity in our society today.

Here is an example of the vicious cycle of refined sugar cravings:

First: Energy rush. Simple sugars go directly into your bloodstream, giving you a temporary high.

Second: There is a pancreatic panic. You may be feeling good, but your high blood sugar is causing your pancreas to scream "DANGER!" There is an enormous response from your pancreas. It dumps huge amounts of insulin into your blood, bringing your blood sugar level down again.

Third: This rush of insulin causes a fast crash. Blood sugar levels swing too low too fast, leading to the sugar blues (leaving one with fatigue and irritability and perhaps a hyperactive response).

You are trapped in a sugar rush cycle. Your energy crash will stimulate your need for another sugar rush to elevate your energy to normalcy. The vicious cycle continues…

There are long-term health hazards associated with refined sugar. Remember, sugar depletes your body of essential minerals and B vitamins. Refined sugar is actually a stripped carbohydrate. When sugar cane—the raw material for sugar—is turned into refined sugar, it is depleted of minerals and nutritional elements. Eating a depleted or stripped carbohydrate forces your body to use its own vitamins and minerals for digestion. Over time, excessive consumption of refined sugars can lead to nutritional deficiencies and serious problems like **osteoporosis**, gum disease and arthritis.

Your body can't produce enough digestive enzymes without the right balance of minerals and B vitamins. Compensating for your sweet tooth by consuming extra healthy foods may be a losing battle since your body is no longer digesting or assimilating food efficiently. **This is another real challenge for children with hyperactivity, since they are already consuming food that is nutritionally stripped.**

Notice

☑ **Eating sugar puts stress on digestion**

☑ **Poor digestion can lead to allergies**

☑ **Sugar consumption results in poor health**

Sweeteners To Avoid

☑ What about other refined sugars? **Brown sugar** is simply refined sugar that is sprayed with molasses to make it appear more whole. **Turbinado sugar** gives the illusion of health, but is just one step away from white sugar. Tubinado is made from 95 percent sucrose (table sugar). It skips only the final filtration stage of sugar refining, resulting in little difference in nutritional value.

☑ **Corn syrup** is found everywhere. It is used in everything from bouillon cubes to spaghetti sauce and even in some "natural" juices. Corn syrup processed from cornstarch is almost as sweet as refined sugar and is absorbed quickly by your blood. Corn-derived sweeteners pose other problems: they often contain high levels of pesticide residues that are genetically modified and are common allergy producers. This is a cheap and plentiful sweetener often used in soft drinks, candy and baked goods. Corn syrup is very similar to refined sugar in composition as well as effect.

☑ **Aspartame**, which is a common synthetic sweetener, affects the nervous system and brain in a very negative way. Aspartame is made from two proteins, or amino acids, which gives it its super sweetness. Aspartame has many harmful effects: behavior changes in children, headaches, dizziness, epileptic-like seizures and bulging of the eyes to name a few. Aspartame is an

---

"excitotoxin", a substance that over stimulates neurons and causes them to die suddenly (as though they were excited to death). One of the last steps of aspartame metabolism is formaldehyde. The next time you consume diet soda, think. You are literally embalming yourself.

☑ **Sucrose** is found in white sugar and maple syrup. Sucrose requires very little digestion and provides instant energy followed by plummeting blood sugar levels. It stresses the entire body system.

☑ **Glucose** is also called dextrose. When combined with sucrose, glucose subjects your blood sugar to the same up and downs. In whole food form—in starches like beans and whole grain breads; they are also rich in soluble fiber—glucose takes longer to digest, resulting in more balanced energy.

☑ **Sorbitol, Mannitol & Zylitol** are synthetic sugar alcohols. Although these can cause less of an insulin jump in glucose to sugar, many people suffer gastric distress. You see these sugars listed as ingredients in foods.

☑ **Unrefined cane juice.** This is sugarcane in crystal form. Nothing more, nothing less. Unrefined cane juice is brown and granulated, contains 85 percent to 96.5 percent sucrose, and retains all of sugarcane's vitamins, minerals and other nutrients. Cane juice has a slightly stronger flavor and less intense sweetness than white sugar. Look for the brand names Sucanat® and Florida Crystals®.

☑ **Crystalline fructose.** This refined simple sugar has the same molecular structure as fruit sugar. It's almost twice as sweet as white sugar, yet releases glucose into the bloodstream much more slowly. Extra sugar gets stored in your liver as glycogen instead of continuing to flood your bloodstream. Thus, crystalline fructose appeals to diabetics and hypoglycemics.

Star Sweeteners

The Best of the Naturals

Become sugar savvy! The term "natural," as applied to sweeteners, can mean many things. The sweeteners recommended below will provide you with steady energy because they take a long time to digest. Natural choices offer rich flavors, vitamins and minerals, without the ups and downs of refined sugars.

Sugar substitutes were actually the natural sweeteners of days past, especially honey and maple syrup. Stay away from man-made artificial sweeteners including aspartame and any of the "sugar alcohols" (names ending in "ol"). In health food stores, be alert for sugars disguised as "evaporated cane juice" or "cane juice crystals." These can still cause problems, regardless what the health food store manager tells you. My patients have seen huge improvements by changing their sugar choices.

☑ **Brown rice syrup.** Your bloodstream absorbs this balanced syrup, high in maltose and complex carbohydrates, slowly and steadily. Brown rice syrup is a natural for baked goods and hot drinks: it adds subtle sweetness and a rich, butterscotch-like flavor. To get sweetness from starchy brown rice, the magic ingredients are enzymes, but the actual process varies depending on the syrup manufacturer. "Malted" syrups use whole, sprouted barley to create a balanced sweetener. Choose these syrups to make tastier muffins and cakes. Cheaper, sweeter rice syrups use isolated enzymes and are a bit harder on blood sugar levels. For a healthy treat, drizzle gently heated rice syrup over popcorn to make natural caramel corn. Store in a cool, dry place.

☑ **Devansoy**™ is the brand name for powdered brown rice sweetener, which contains the same complex carbohydrates as brown rice syrup and a natural plant flavoring.

☑ **Barley malt syrup.** This sweetener is made much like rice syrup, but it uses sprouted barley to turn grain starches into a complex sweetener that is digested slowly. Use barley malt syrup to add molasses-like flavor and light sweetness to beans, cookies, muffins and cakes. Store in cool, dry place.

☑ **Amasake** is an ancient, oriental whole grain sweetener made from cultured brown rice. It has a thick, pudding-like consistency. Baked goods benefit from amasake's subtle sweetness, moisture and leavening power.

☑ **Stevia** is a sweet South American herb that has been used safely by many cultures for centuries. Extensive scientific studies back-up these ancient claims to safety. However, the FDA has approved it only when labeled as a dietary supplement, not as a sweetener. Advocates consider stevia to be one of the healthiest sweeteners as well as a tonic to heal the skin. Stevia is 150 to 400 times sweeter than white sugar, has no calories and can actually regulate blood sugar levels. Unrefined stevia has a molasses-like flavor; refined stevia (popular in Japan) has less flavor and nutrients.

☑ **Fruitsource®.** This brand-name sweetener combines the sweetness of grape juice concentrate with the complex carbohydrates of brown rice syrup. *FruitSource* is light amber in color and 80 percent as sweet as white sugar. *Liquid Plus*, a similar product, better matches the sweetness of white sugar. Look for *FruitSource* in liquid and granulated form. Whichever form you choose, the options are better for your blood sugar than refined sugar!

☑ **Whole fruit.** For baking, try fruit purees, dried fruit and cooked fruit sauces or butters. The less water remaining in a fruit, the more concentrated its flavor and sugar content. You'll find fiber and naturally-balanced nutrients in whole fruits like apples, bananas and apricots. To add mild sweetness and moisture to baked goods, mix in the magic of mashed winter squashes, sweet potatoes and carrots!

☑ **Fructose** in whole foods provides balanced energy.

☑ **Honey.** It takes one bee an entire lifetime to produce a single tablespoon of honey from flower nectar. But that small amount goes a long way! Honey is mostly made of glucose and fructose and is up to twice as sweet as white sugar. Honey enters the bloodstream rapidly. Look for raw honey, which still contains some vitamins, minerals, enzymes and pollen. Honeys vary in color (according to their flower source) and range in strength from mild clover to strong orange blossom. A benefit of eating honey produced in your geographical region is that it may reduce hay fever and allergy symptoms by bolstering your natural immunity. Note: raw honey can lead to a toxic, sometimes fatal form of botulism in children under one. Limit honey consumption, as it results in similar results as sucrose.

☑ **Maltose** is the primary sugar in brown rice and barley malt syrups. Maltose is a complex sugar that is digested slowly. It is the sugar with "staying power."

☑ **Maple Syrup.** It takes about 10 gallons of maple sap to produce 1 gallon of maple syrup. Like honey, a little goes a long way. Maple syrup is roughly 65 percent sucrose and contains small amounts of trace minerals. Maple syrup has a rich taste and is absorbed fairly quickly into the bloodstream. Select real maple syrup that has no added corn syrup. Also, look for syrups that come from organic producers who don't use formaldehyde to prolong sap flow. Grade A syrups come from the first tapping: they range in color from light to dark amber. Grade B syrups come from the last tapping; they have more minerals and a stronger flavor and color.

☑ **Date sugar.** This sweetener is made from dried, ground dates, is light brown and has a sugary texture. Date sugar retains many naturally-occurring vitamins and minerals, is 65 percent sucrose and has a fairly rapid effect on blood sugar. Use it in baking instead of brown sugar, but reduce your baking time or temperature in order to prevent premature browning. Store in a cool, dry place.

☑ **Concentrated fruit juice.** All concentrates are not created equally. Highly-refined juice sweeteners are labeled "modified." These sweeteners, similar to white sugar, have lost both their fruit flavor and their nutrients. Better choices are fruit concentrates that have been evaporated in a vacuum. These retain rich fruit flavors and aromas and many vitamins and minerals. Carefully read labels on cereal, cookie, jelly and beverage containers, then choose products with the highest percentage of real fruit juice. Beware of white grape juice concentrates that aren't organic; their pesticide residues can be high!

☑ **Blackstrap molasses.** Molasses, a by-product of sugar production, is a highly-processed simple sugar that enters the bloodstream rapidly. Molasses may also contain chemical residues associated with the growing and refining of white sugar. If you grew up on conventional molasses, your taste buds may have to adjust to the softer bite of **blackstrap molasses, which contains high amounts of balancing minerals such as calcium, iron, potassium, magnesium, zinc, copper and chromium.** Use it as a sweetener in cakes, pies and cookies. Barbados molasses is sweeter and more syrupy than blackstrap; it is perfect for baking but lacks blackstrap's minerals. **(Note: Diabetics should not use any type of molasses.)**

Sugar Substitution

Amount Indicates the Equivalent of 1 Cup of White Sugar

Sweetener	Amount	Liquid Reduction	Suggested Use
Honey	1/2 - 2/3 cup	1/4 cup	All-purpose
Maple syrup	1/2 - 3/4 cup	1/4 cup	Baking & desserts
Maple sugar	1/2 - 1/3 cup	None	Baking & candies
Barley malt syrup	1 - 1 1/2 cups	1/2 cup	Breads & baking
Rice syrup	1 - 1/3 cups	1/2 cup	Baking & cakes
Date sugar	2/3 cup	None	Breads & baking
Blackstrap Molasses	1/2 cup	1/4 cup	Breads & baking
Fruit juice concentrate	1 cup	1/3 cuup	All-purpose
Stevia	1 tsp/cup of water	1 cup	Baking

(Note: If you have a serious blood sugar regulation problem, such as diabetes or hypoglycemia, see your Health Care Practitioner to determine the type and amount of sweeteners your body can handle.)

See Recipes in Chapter 19

13

Fantastic Flax

Common Questions Regarding Flaxseed Oil

Does my recommendation to supplement your diet with one or two tablespoons of flaxseed oil per day pique your curiosity? Most health authorities tell people to restrict their intake of fats and oils. However, I believe my recommendation makes perfectly good sense for good health. Our patients regularly report to us the benefits of flax, most notably stabilized, healthy cholesterol or triglyceride levels. While it is true Americans should not consume more than 30 percent of daily calories as fats, a lack of the dietary essential fatty acids (EFAs) plays a significant role in the development of many chronic and degenerative diseases such as heart disease, arthritis, cancer and strokes.

Q. *How common is essential fatty acid insufficiency?*

A. Some experts estimate that as much as 80 percent of the United States population fails to consume an adequate quantity of essential fatty acids. This dietary insufficiency presents a serious health threat to Americans. Nearly 100 percent of my patients initially had never heard of flax oil prior to their initial visit to my office. Essential fatty acids are important for the regulation many bodily functions including:

☑ Inflammation, pain and swelling

☑ Blood pressure

☑ Heart function

☑ Gastrointestinal function and secretions

☑ Kidney function and fluid balance

☑ Blood clotting and platelet aggregation

☑ *Allergic response*

☑ *Nerve transmission*

☑ Steroid production and hormone synthesis

Q. *How do I know if I am deficient in essential fatty acids?*

A. The signs and symptoms of essential fatty acid deficiency vary. A fatty acid deficiency can be quite obvious or may be somewhat hard to detect as the symptoms are typically attributed to other causes.

Symptoms typical of, but not exclusive to, EFA deficiency

☑ **Aching, sore joints**	☑ **Fatigue, malaise, lackluster energy**
☑ **Angina, chest pain**	
☑ **Arthritis**	☑ **Forgetfulness**
☑ **Constipation**	☑ **Frequent colds and sickness**
☑ **Cracked nails**	☑ **High blood pressure**
☑ **Depression**	☑ **History of cardiovascular disease**
☑ **Dry mucous membranes, tear ducts, mouth, vagina**	☑ **Immune system weakness**
	☑ **Indigestion, gas, bloating**
☑ **Dry, lifeless hair**	☑ **Lack of endurance**
☑ **Dry skin**	☑ **Lack of motivation**

Over 60 unhealthful conditions have now been shown to benefit from essential fatty acid supplementation.

Some health conditions linked to low EFA levels

☑ Acne	☑ Elevated cholesterol levels
☑ AIDS	☑ Heart disease
☑ Allergies	☑ High blood pressure
☑ Alzheimer's disease	☑ Hyperactivity
☑ Arthritis	☑ Lupus
☑ Attention Deficit Disorder	☑ Multiple sclerosis
☑ Breast cancer and other cancers	☑ ODD
☑ Depression	☑ Obesity
☑ Eczema	☑ Psoriasis

Q. *What is the preferred material to package flaxseed oil, plastic or glass?*

A. An opaque plastic container made of high-density polyethylene (HDPE) is the preferred material for packaging and protecting flaxseed oil from light. The HDPE material is fully approved by U.S. and Canadian governments for these purposes and has an untarnished record for health and safety. Independent laboratory analyses conducted by responsible organic oil producers have resulted in absolutely no migration of the HDPE material into the oil they contain. Even amber pharmaceutical-grade glass allows over five different light frequencies to penetrate the bottle with the potential to destroy the benefits of the oil.

Q. *Are there any side effects common to taking flaxseed oil?*

A. Since flaxseed oil is a food source, side effects from supplementation with flaxseed oil are highly uncommon. The possibility does always exist, just as with any food source, that someone may react unfavorably with the oil. For some individuals this may be a transitory effect, whereas simply reducing the dosage should relieve any problem. Oily skin is a possible side effect and may be a sign of liver congestion from a B6 deficiency. It will take time for your body to process the extra oil. For any others, simply discontinue usage or seek the advice of a nutritionally-oriented practitioner.

Q. *What is high-lignan flaxseed oil?*

A. In addition to their high level of Omega 3 fatty acid, flaxseeds are also the most abundant source of lignans. Lignans are special compounds that demonstrate some rather impressive health benefits, including positive effects in relieving menopausal hot flashes, as well as promoting anti-cancer, antibacterial, antifungal and antiviral activity. Adding some of these lignans back to the oil produces high lignan flaxseed oil. However, even regular flaxseed oil is very high in lignans and is the second richest source behind whole flaxseeds.

Never Heat Flax Oil

14

Unmasking Vitamins

Supplement Protocol

There is a HUGE difference between synthetic and natural vitamin supplements. Often supplements may cause health problems. If you and/or your family are taking supplements and have noticed no change in health response, please try the types of supplements that I am suggesting.

You may, in fact, buy your own supplements via a network marketing company...Yet while there are excellent companies out there, it comes down to results.

Supplements are another component of "media nutrients." Various companies advertise *"'specialized' or high dosage supplements."* There are many sources of supplements. Some are excellent; others are quite poor. You may, in fact, buy your own supplements via a network marketing company. That's great. Yet while there are excellent companies out there, it comes down to results.

Do not believe everything you see on T.V. Ask your natural health care advisor for assistance. Vitamins/minerals/herbs have become convenience, synthetic foods. I have patients who are taking bags of supplements and still feel miserable. There are medical providers today who have found it very profitable to be the spokesperson for a vitamin/herb line. Some have developed their own line of vitamins (some of which is proven "junk"). Not all "allopathic" physicians turned "natural" physicians understand simple physiology.

Further, you do not get what you pay for, either. There are a lot of high-cost products that are useless and even harmful.

Vitamins—The Most Processed "Food"

Take this quick and simple quiz: What is the most processed food you consume? Is it donuts? How about margarine? Is it a hot dog? The answer to all these is **no**. Unless you are taking vitamins made from food, the most processed foods you probably consume are your synthetic vitamin supplements.

> **Synthetic vitamins are so processed that it is impossible to find any semblance of any isolated synthetic vitamin in nature.**

Synthetic vitamins are so processed that it is impossible to find any semblance of any isolated synthetic vitamin in nature. I challenge anyone to locate a source for a pure, fractionalized, isolated vitamin anywhere in nature's food chain. For example, try to find a plant that contains only vitamin B1 or B3. It's impossible. All genuinely natural vitamins occur in complexes containing not just the isolated vitamin but its naturally-occurring counterparts as well.

Almost all supplementary vitamins, including those from the health food store, are produced in laboratories. In fact, huge pharmaceutical conglomerates produce most supplementary vitamins. These are not made from plants, organic matter or any sort of *food*. Instead, they are *created* from a base of petroleum (as in motor oil) or tar (as in coal).

Fancy Names

The truth is that almost all vitamin "manufacturers" are simply vitamin bottlers. They get their raw vitamins from one of a handful of manufacturers. For a selling point, the bottler puts on a label that infers that these vitamins are organic or natural. Of course, this is *false*. "Organic" and "natural" mean *absolutely nothing* on the label of a vitamin bottle and certainly does not describe the ingredients used in the product.

Truly Natural and Organic

Nature intended for nutrition from the soil to be organic, ready for human consumption as with plants. Plants chelate, or produce, organic nutrition for us. Animals eat some plants and they, too, may play a part in the vitamin and mineral food chain as nature intended.

When nutrition is concentrated in this manner, it is in its perfect form: loaded with the proper nutrients, trace elements and enzymes which are easily digested and readily assimilated by the human body. There is no need for your body to break down or fractionalize nutrients. Likewise, there is no need for your body to "reassemble" the proper nutritional complex because it is already perfect.

Are Organic and Synthetic the Same?

Those who would have you believe that there is absolutely no difference between natural and synthetic are misleading you. And with today's labeling laws, I can understand why. As stated previously, most vitamins labeled "organic" or "natural" contain synthetic vitamins due to some regulations. Perhaps a bit of stale food material is used so that the label can say "organic" or "natural." Even in such cases, the *product remains purely synthetic.*

...it is impossible to find a vitamin B fraction like B1 isolated in any plant.

Also realize that when it comes to comparing a vitamin **fraction** (like one of the isolated B vitamins), there is very little difference between that made in the laboratory and that found in nature. The difference shows up in the nutritional *complex* that contains any vitamin fraction. For example, it is impossible to find a vitamin B fraction like B1 isolated in any plant. So, when you get a B1 vitamin made from plants, it will naturally contain the other B vitamin components as well as all other nutrients that **surround vitamin B1 naturally**.

If your body used vitamins in fractions (i.e., B1, B3, B6) then there would be some truth that the synthetic and organic act identically in your body. The ridiculous adage "your body doesn't know the difference" is an insult to your intelligence.

Homeowners: If you were normally using a fuel mixture of pure gasoline and oil in your power weedwacker, and you decided to add only the finest of pure gasoline without the oil, would it make a difference in how the weedwacker would run? Cooks: If a recipe calls for whole-wheat flour, and you add only a fraction of the wheat flour (like the bran), will the baked product taste differently?

> **...real, organic vitamins...can only be *concentrated* from plants; they cannot be artificially produced.**

The same is true with real, organic vitamins. These can only be *concentrated* from plants; they **cannot be artificially produced**. When you concentrate nutrients from plants, you will necessarily have a product that is a *proper blend* of nutrients (as nature intended). Therefore, there is a limit in the *quantities* of each nutrient that can be concentrated into one tablet.

A Dead Giveaway

If it were possible to concentrate the maximum amount of vitamin C from nature's most vitamin C-rich plants, you would only be able to fit a small amount of this vitamin C into a tablet. The reason is that a little vitamin A, some bio-flavonoids, some trace elements, and a few enzymes would be present with the vitamin C. This is absolutely the way it should be. It is the reason your body will utilize this vitamin C a hundred times better than it could ascorbic acid (synthetic vitamin C).

Herein lies the rub—and the dead giveaway. Even using plants that are richest in vitamin C, the most you can cram into one tablet is maybe 30 mg. Therefore, to produce a 1000 mg. vitamin C that is labeled "all natural and organic" would require a tablet *larger than a golf ball*.

The Synthetic Reaction

The fact is that a synthetic vitamin is any vitamin with a more than 30 mg of vitamin C, more than 15 IUs of vitamin E, more than 5,000 IUs of vitamin A and so on. Don't get me wrong. This does not mean that all synthetic vitamins are bad, because I use some synthetics in my practice. However, *nothing* works better in the human body than truly *organic* nutrients (as we have now truthfully defined).

Many people feel that they get a genuine "lift" or "rush" from taking high-potency, synthetic vitamins. This is often true. However, the rush may not be from any rapid improvement in body functions. Rather, it is usually from an adrenal gland activity related to your body's reacting to an unnatural, high-dose, synthetic product. Their ingestion will involve the liver, pancreas, adrenals and other glands and organs. In other words, the body has *to work*, breaking down or reassembling synthetic nutrients into compounds that are "usable." In fact, it is not unusual for high dose synthetic nutrients to **cause nutrient deficiencies**. Here's what can happen.

> **...it is not unusual for high dose synthetic nutrients to cause nutrient deficiencies.**

Deficiencies from Synthetic Vitamins

If you take too much zinc, your body will naturally become deficient in copper and iron. In nature, these three minerals work in combination. Stores of copper and iron from your body may be needed to balance the intake of too much zinc.

The same thing can happen with the B vitamins. Taking too much of one synthetic vitamin B fraction can induce deficiencies of the entire B complex. Your body will call upon its B vitamin stores to help balance out the huge amount of one vitamin B fraction. Since vitamin B is a water-soluble nutrient with little surplus stored in the body, a deficiency can result rather easily.

Common Sense

When you take vitamins—whether synthetic or organic—you are usually eating food at the same time. And there is no doubt in any scientific community that nutrients from *food* are best. However, given the state of our soils and food chain, it is no longer possible for most people to get all the nutrients they need from a daily diet. However, given the facts about nature, food and nutrition, supplemental nutrients are best utilized and most effective when they are made *from food*.

> ... supplemental nutrients are best utilized and most effective when they are made *from food*.

No matter what you read or are told, there is an *immense difference* between these two types of products. Forget all the scientific explanations. After more than 50 years of clinical testing, nutritional doctors and healers have proven outright that organic works best. If you are really sick, you need nutrients that won't tax your body, but rather support your bodily systems and replenish nutritional stores so that your body can heal.

If you are wondering why you are still unhealthy even after taking vitamins, ask yourself three questions: Is my nutritional program individualized for *me*? What type of products am I taking? Are *hydrogenated oils* the first ingredient in the product I am taking? Remember to read labels; even vitamins can have unhealthy ingredients. When it comes to your health, this is not the time to buy the cheapest products with the highest dosage.

Patients are often confused about supplements. They consume huge amounts yet continue to deteriorate. Recently, I treated a patient who purchased supplements from a nationally recognized authority. She developed "liver spots" on her hands after using this product for many years. We took her off the product and her skin cleared.

Easy Steps To Supplement Success

Low Dosage, Cold Processed (Easily Assimilated & Absorbable) Minerals, Flax and B vitamins are Necessary for the Program.

I have found that patients who are taking supplements—those bought through the mail, the internet, at the mall or pharmacy—are still facing major challenges. They aren't receiving optimum results from the supplements they currently use. I utilize several products successfully in my practice that are available to natural health care providers.

Are all supplements created equal? Use products that get results: supplements that are low-dosage, whole-food complexes (see product inquiry information). More than likely, you'll be able to find these supplements at a health food store or a natural health care provider. Synthetic, high-dosage, nutritionally-devitalized vitamins can lead to your child's diminished of health and hyperactivity. Be wary of "All Natural" labels.

1. **Flax.** 1 tablespoon daily per 100 lbs. You can take this anytime, with or without meals. It can also be added to food. Do not heat flax. Store the bottle upside down so the lingans can be at the mouth of the bottle.

   a. **Salmon** (fish oil). Take one capsule right before bed for 18 days. Salmon capsules can also be taken on those days when the individual on the program eats hydrogenated fats, sugar or dairy. You do not need to use this every time you deviate, but we have seen success with adding this protocol. The salmon oil does not need to go through the steps to become the final step (prostaglandin) like flax, in Chart # 3.

2. **B vitamin.** I have my patients take six daily the first month, two with each meal. Three daily is adequate after that. Any low-dosage, cold-process whole food B vitamin is proper. There are many brands and popular names. If you are taking supplements and there is no behavioral improvement, try another product. Do not use high dosage mega B vitamins.

3. **B6.** Use three daily per day for the first month. Continue with one daily for the entire program.

4. **Minerals.** Use whole food complex with alfalfa and kelp as the primary ingredients. Signs of mineral deficiency can include salt craving, bright light irritation, bowed legs, night cramps, growing pains, migrating pains, difficulty in swallowing, menses cramps, "mottled teeth," frequent fevers, nail chewing, etc. Proper mineral consumption is often overlooked, but a key to good health. Minerals act like spark plugs. You can consume food that is processed which you think is good, but actually leads to a breakdown in the body. Minerals are needed for proper fat metabolism. I also encourage my patients to use a mineral "salt product" called Celtic Sea Salt. The salt normally used in homes, restaurants, etc., is sodium chloride. This is very toxic and can irritate the body. I would encourage you to use the Celtic Sea Salt liberally on your food. It is an excellent mineral.

Please Note

I am not making specific milligram suggestions for each supplement. I use low-dosage, whole-food source supplements.

15

Beyond Antibiotics

Experience is valuable when making observations. Many of America's children have been on one or two programs of antibiotics or medication for emotional or behavioral challenges, sometimes even more. It is not uncommon to find children on regular "maintenance" dosages of general or wide-spectrum antibiotics for as many as four years. Keeping children on antibiotics does not give the child's own immune system an opportunity to perform what it was designed to do. Physicians should preach on lifestyle modification.

While wide-spectrum antibiotics are designed to minimize and eliminate unhealthy bacteria, they also keep the healthy bacteria in check, precipitating yeast overgrowth. Yeast overgrowth leads to a variety of symptoms and conditions, including hyperactivity. Your child and you will continue to crave sugar, which feeds the yeast and continues the cycle of yeast overgrowth and toxins being released into the system. The cycle must be broken. First, you must change your current lifestyle. If you do not, you will continue to be dependent on antibiotics.

I am not saying never take antibiotics. But anything less than prudence weakens the immune system and leads to taking antibiotics on a continuous basis. The recent media blast of "super bugs" resulting from antibiotics misuse should alarm you enough to do something different.

The utilization of antibiotics is a part of the Catch-22 which often precipitates the entire problem. Children are trapped within a cycle of being raised by parents who work (meaning fewer children are breastfed, and are introduced to liquid, solid foods and milk that are inappropriate for the body). This then sets-up an allergic reaction, and allows undigested food to travel through the body, causing chronic infections, and ultimately resulting in the use of antibiotics that kill both good and bad bacteria.

If you do consume antibiotics, it is essential that you replace the flora in the body through probiotic replanting.

If you do consume antibiotics, it is essential that you replace the flora in the body through probiotic replanting.

Probiotics

Probiotics are a group of friendly bacteria that help us stay healthy. They include Lactobacillus Acidophilus and Lactobacillus Bifidus and other Bifidobacteria. These bacteria, which are found in yogurt, were first identified about 100 years ago. In 1908, a scientist named Metchkinoff recommended the daily consumption of yogurt because he felt it promoted good health and prolonged life.

Since the turn of the century, preparations containing these friendly bacteria have been used by physicians and nonphysicians alike to treat complaints ranging from constipation and diarrhea to skin problems. One patient reported, "I've tried various remedies for my bloating, constipation, abdominal pain and recurrent vaginitis. Finally I found that by taking probiotics regularly, I'm better than I've been in years. Of course, I also have sharply reduced my intake of sugar."

Lactobacillus Acidophilus and Lactobacillus Bifidus (and other Bifidobacteria) are perhaps the best-known probiotics. Preparations containing these organisms can be found in health food stores and pharmacies. A third friendly bacterium,

Streptococcus Faecium, has also been found to be effective in curbing the growth of harmful bacteria in the digestive tract.

During the past decade, several conferences have been held on the candida/human interaction. Almost without exception, both professionals and nonprofessionals described their use of probiotic products for persons with yeast-related health problems.

One of the best discussions about probiotics was in the book *Childhood Ear Infections*, by Dr. Michael A. Schmidt. Dr. Schmidt lists 15 beneficial functions performed by Lactobacillus Acidophilus and Bifidobacteria in the intestinal tract. Here are a few of them:

> Contribute to "germ-eating" activity of some of the body's immune cells; produce organic acids and hydrogen peroxide, which kill invading microbes; **make important B vitamins**; allow for better utilization of nutrients from foods; prevent the fungus Candida Albicans from forming invasive germ tubes; inhibit the growth of Candida Albicans in the digestive tract and vagina.

When asked the following question, "Do you use plain Lactobacillus Acidophilus or a combination product?" Jeffrey Bland, Ph.D., responded:

> *"I think we all recognize that the most important criteria for activity of probiotic substances is that there must be an adequate number of live organisms, they must be reasonably resistant to oxgall (bile) and they must be able to adhere to the gastrointestinal epithelium (intestinal wall). If any one of these three criteria is not present, then the activity of the product is limited.*
>
> *At our center, we start patients on preparations of Lactobacillus Acidophilus. If we don't get a response, we try Bifidobacteria. So they get them*

both. I don't think there's any harm in giving these products in combination form because they're combined in the intestinal tract at all times."

Dr. Crooks, author of *The Yeast Connection*, states:

"You can find a number of probiotic products in your health food store. I recommend them as a nutritional supplement for my patients—especially those who are taking or have taken broad-spectrum antibiotic drugs."

Donna Gates, in her book *The Body Ecology Diet* details the benefits of Kefir. Kefir is a cultured and microbial rich food that helps restore the inner ecology of the body. This can also help your body to maintain a natural balance of bacteria.

16

Subluxation

Nerve Interference

Your nervous system is the body's computer network. It links everything together. This is a vital link that will help not only your child's health but your own as well. Natural health care providers, including naturopaths, osteopaths and chiropractors, have utilized spinal correction since the 1800s. Medical practitioners have no formal training in this area. Their focus is on the pharmaceutical approach to treating the disease. All health care providers have their niche. If the power is off to your refrigerator, you could put ice packs in it every four hours to keep it cool and do that for years, but wouldn't it be easier to flip the switch that would turn the power on to the motor? Yes.

Nutritional modification, behavior management and medication are not the entire answer. Spinal subluxation correction with a holistic pactitioner plus nutritional supplementation is an important part of the process. You can consume nutrients, but if your nervous system is not functioning optimally, your body will not function at top performance. Your nervous system controls the function of your body.

What is Subluxation?

Subluxation is a condition brought about when a spinal bone displaces and/or presses on nerves that carry information from the brain through the spinal cord to organs. Subluxations can start from a traumatic birth process or injury shortly after birth. Children can have subluxations without experiencing spinal pain. This is very important to understand.

> **Subluxation, pressure on the spinal nerves, literally stops the body's ability to heal itself.**

An optimally functioning spine equals optimum health. It is commonly accepted by health care practitioners that these displacements and/or subluxations of the spine can stop your body from sending vital healing information. Many, if not all, of the common health problems that we learn to live with *can be caused by these subluxations*.

What Can Cause a Subluxation?

Subluxation can be caused by a variety of things: poor posture, poor sleeping habits, diet, motor vehicle accidents and poor working conditions. Slips, falls, strains and the birth process itself can be a reason for subluxation. This is why it is very important that you and everyone in your family have a postural subluxation check-up.

Subluxations can be precipitated by what we eat. Patients who consume dairy, sweet fruits, sugar, liver-congesting and adrenal-stressing food, have chronic left neck, left shoulder and migrating joint pain. This can be explained by food particle sensitivity, visceral somatic (organ nerve reflexes) and mineral imbalances. You become what you eat. Try your own experiment: eat no sugar and dairy for one week, then start with one banana, raisins or grapes. See what happens. I guarantee if the banana doesn't do it, try chocolate, soda, ice cream, cookies or cotton candy. Whatever you love. You will get left neck, shoulder or mid-back pain. This cycle affects neck alignment, which has a major impact on body function.

Although medication sometimes manages conditions, you need to investigate all the reasons why your child is not in optimal health, including a spinal check-up. You cannot forget the food and only have spinal corrections. I have patients and friends whose children have regular spinal check-ups, but their condition is not improved because their diet is not altered.

A New Approach for a New Century

All body functions are controlled by the brain sending and receiving messages over nerves. Vertebrae (the bones in your back) fit together so that the nerve supply controlled and directed by your brain may filter down your spinal cord and out over your nerves. This healing information is responsible for growth, repair and healing in your entire body. When vertebrae are out of their natural alignment, nerves become stretched or twisted (commonly referred to as a nerve "pinch"), causing the vital communication system in the body to be disrupted.

Seek out a health care provider who specializes in the detection and correction of subluxations.

Seek out a health care provider who specializes in the detection and correction of subluxations. This is done by laying hands on your back and gently lining up the vertebrae in their natural position. This process may take weeks or months, depending on the amount of misalignment. Health may then be restored throughout the body and healing can take place. As your body heals, the symptoms begin to diminish. When vertebral subluxations disrupt this vital communication system, one or more parts of the body may begin to fail which contributes to a decline in health in general. That's how vertebral subluxations can lead to various neurological, emotional and physical disorders like attention deficit disorder or hyperactivity. That's why subluxation practitioners are concerned with restoring normal body function.

There are various health care providers who manipulate and correct spinal subluxations. However, if you are going to be placing your child under the care of an individual practitioner, I would encourage you to find a highly-skilled, trained spinal adjustor. **You want a subluxation specialist.** Be aware, there are health care providers attempting to correct subluxation without sufficient training, including, but not limited to, medical physicians, physical therapists and massage therapists. I would definitely interview and have a conversation with any health care provider that treats your child.

Success With Spinal Corrective Care

For many years, doctors who remove subluxation have reported success with hyperactivity, ADD, ADHD and ODD. If children with attention deficit disorders can benefit from subluxation correction— gaining improved attention span, controlled activity level and general well being—it's reasonable to assume that even the average child would benefit by improved health and well-being. **Your child will have a better opportunity to have optimum health by having subluxations corrected throughout childhood.**

> If children with attention deficit disorders can benefit from subluxation correction...it's reasonable to assume that even the average child would benefit by improved health and well-being.

Subluxation correction is a natural approach to health care. It does not try to stimulate or inhibit normal body function. Instead, the health care provider addresses the important relationship between the nervous system and disease. The systemic effect of vertebral subluxations is complex. Many childhood illnesses may be manifested by abnormal body function caused by subluxations. In light of this, your spinal corrective practitioner may be the best doctor to help your child. Children should be monitored regularly (like a routine dental examination) for subluxations to ensure good health.

Posture Tips

A. There are several posture exercises that can help maintain muscle tone and stabilize spinal structure. **The Door Jam Push-Up** is a simple maneuver designed to pull the shoulders back. A forward head position is not a healthy posture alignment.

Stand in a door jam. Raise your hands to shoulder height or above, place the palms on the door jam and lean your body into the doorway. Hold this five seconds. Do three sets of 15 daily.

B. In time you can add **the lay down** or modify as in picture, reverse body trunk curl. It requires a weight bench, picnic table bench or a coffee table. While lying on your back, slide your head/trunk to the end of your support structure. Slide off until you are mid-shoulder blade or lower. Hang your head, shoulders and upper trunk off the edge. Hold for about 30 seconds. Increase your time up to two minutes daily. This is an excellent active maneuver which strengthens the trunk and pulls the upper body backward. Forward body posture puts a pull on the brain, spinal cord and spinal nerves.

C. The last maneuver is **the head glide**. This takes some concentration. Sit with your eyes closed. Slide your head and upper neck straight backward then tilt back slightly. Do not move your shoulders. This is an excellent way to establish and maintain a normal cervical curve. A normal lordotic cervical curve will increase the strength of your spine by a factor of seven. Hold the head position five seconds. Complete three sets of 15 every day. You may feel slight neck pain at first, but this exercise will prevent long-term spinal imbalance and will help minimize the damage caused by subluxation once your subluxations are checked and corrected. Regular exercise maneuvers, like regular spinal checks, are necessary because of the CONSTANT stress gravity relentlessly forces on our body.

You may not experience a miracle after your first visit with the subluxation correcting health care provider. Do not get upset or quit. It may be that your nervous system has been functioning less than optimally for years. Breakdown takes time. Correction takes time. (As an example, teeth develop in improper position over time and will correct to the proper position over time. Skilled dentists can look at a dental x-ray and see which teeth had the most correction years after the correction was established. I use my lower retainer for my teeth; my braces were removed 15 years ago). Your body is in a constant state of breakdown and repair. Repair requires energy and breakdown is effortless.

How Does Subluxation Remove ADHD, etc?

Figure 1	Figure 2	Figure 3

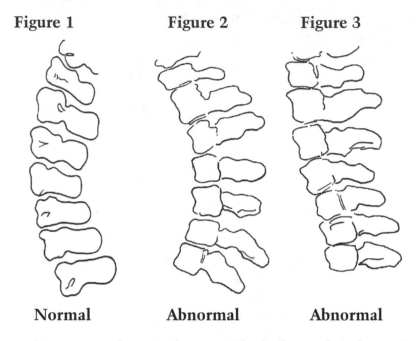

Normal	Abnormal	Abnormal

Figure 1 is a normal cervical curve. The body sends information from the brain down the spinal cord to organs and tissues in the body. Children who are hyperactive or have attention deficit challenges often have an abnormal cervical curve. Our pilot program research shows that our participants had a 10° cervical lordosis curve (the arc of a forward curve) commonly called "kyhpotic" or combination curve when subluxated (normal is 45°). This is often precipitated by a traumatic birth. Did your child have a traumatic birth? Did your child fall off the changing table? Did your child have an injury early on in his or her development? If so, this could be a reason why your child is having these challenges. **We also have seen children who have chronic ear infections and asthma respond tremendously to subluxation care.**

The significance of an abnormal cervical curve is the fact that the child's spinal cord is literally being "choked," *and information going from the brain cells to the tissue cells is interrupted*. Look at your child's posture. If you do not see a forward "C curve" and the child's neck appears to be flat and/or the child has been involved in any type of trauma, they should be checked by a subluxation practitioner.

Subluxation correction has been used to successfully treat children for years. The Chinese have used subluxation removal and spinal manipulation for thousands of years.

Unfortunately, subluxation is an area overlooked by most health care providers and individuals who treat hyperactivity. Subluxation literally stops the body from sending messages from the spinal cord throughout all the organs and tissues. Don't make this mistake! Don't miss a key component in the treatment plan to combat ADHD, ADD or ODD.

NOTES:

17
Supportive Parent's Guide

If you are extremely frustrated and disillusioned, I understand your dilemma. Most patients don't know exactly where to start.

Dealing With Feelings

There is a tremendous amount of tension and frustration in households with a hyperactive child. Parents may be at an exploding point as to how to handle their child's emotional outbreaks. Parents are frustrated and confused by their child's behavior: behavior that is "normal" one moment and totally different the next for no apparent reason. Many parents feel totally helpless. In a recent conversation, one mom imitated for me the shrieking, screaming noises her son makes for no obvious reason. Parents feel that there is no hope and have friends who are just as confused. Parents' emotions are constantly being stretched, and they don't know what to do.

You need to be strong, diplomatic and objective. Hyperactivity is a real condition that improves only by making lifestyle and dietary changes. Everyone is not going to accept change. The child is stressed enough. These real life issues, feelings, thoughts and ideas are a part of your program. You may be frustrated because you have read many articles about hyperactivity, ADD, ADHD and ODD that suggest various supplements, herbs, potions and psychological therapy and counseling, but no improvement is forthcoming.

Look at the process as a return to simplicity. If you follow the simple steps I have outlined, it will get better. Your child will once again return to a normal, more controlled state. A common challenge is what your child should eat. Both parents must agree in order to have a win/win situation. This cannot be a tug of war. *I have seen one parent that is health conscious while the other parent encourages french fries, chips, sodas and ice cream.* This is even more stressful with a blended family where the biological parents are separated. It is hard enough when the child is under the same roof with both biological parents. New relationships with stepparents, boyfriends, girlfriends, in-laws, grandparents, peer pressure, etc., compounds the problem. Sometimes, the demands on our routine are more than most can handle. Financial strain and divorce lead to disrupted relationships with our children. We consume food on the run and rarely eat together. Families are scattered in *numerous* directions.

There is a light at the end of the tunnel. You need to make a few changes and add a few supplements. These are small steps to calmness and peace. **There is a light at the end of the tunnel.** Relax. Take a few deep breaths and know…it will get better!

Reality Check

There are a variety of reasons why there are hyperactive children taking Ritalin, Adderall and other behavior modifying medications. I have explored this in detail with patients, family, teachers and friends of varied backgrounds. Lack of knowledge on how the body works is a leading factor in behavioral disorders. Educated patients (parents) make wise choices. Parental involvement in a child's life is essential. Teachers share with me the heartache they have for children that are literally on their own. It is frustrating for all involved with a child who has behavioral challenges. Parents, please apply the principles you've learned in this book and make the necessary changes. Teachers, friends and relatives, be supportive and patient. You all need to communicate honestly, quietly and with love to the child. Create an alliance so everyone wins. I have heard of reports where parents needed attorneys to get their children off drugs and into different environments. My goal is for the child to live a happy, healthy, normal life with the least amount of stress.

Yes, there are various protocols for children, including a variety of drugs and behavior modification techniques. But logically there are many factors, including the high incidence of divorce, lack of family time and the rush of life, that contribute to this dilemma. Families with biological parents at home who spend time with their children cannot escape behavioral problems if the kids eat SUGAR, DAIRY and HYDRO-GENATED FATS. Many children who eat this way have problems with or without parental support.

Parents need to change as well.

Parents need to change as well. This is not always easy. *It is okay for the children, but often the adults continue their unhealthy diet. Children will trust your behavior toward lifestyle changes. If you are positive and motivated, then they will be positive and motivated, too.*

The information presented here is also prevention-oriented in nature. We see individuals who choose logical, natural health care choices and do not have children with behavioral problems initiated by food imbalances. Yes, we all have day-to-day dilemmas in personal family matters, but the one consistent overriding reason for hyperactivity is directly related to **what we consume and how our nervous system functions.** Patients who practiced natural therapeutics from the beginning (or even prior to the delivery of the child) do not have diminished states of health that lead to chronic infections, repeated antibiotic use and hyperactivity. An ounce of prevention *is* worth a pound of cure.

When you finish reading this book, discuss its contents with your inner circle of friends. It is important—especially if they are contemplating having a child—that they make necessary and appropriate lifestyle choices devoid of processed foods and chemicals.

Why Do You Need To Change?

A study by Dr. Egger, showed that of 76 selected overactive children on a hypoallergenic diet, 62 (82 percent) improved and 21 (28 percent) achieved normalcy. It is quite obvious that altering the diet can definitely make improvements in a child's overall health. Similarly, the problems with which adults suffer can also be directly linked to poor diet.

Juvenile delinquents drink three times more milk than non-delinquents, consume 30-100% more sugar and live on coffee and packaged sweets.

Barbara Reed, introduced in the book *Food Allergy and Nutrition Revolution*, is a probation officer from Cuyahoga Falls, Ohio, who herself struggled with nutritional problems. She has worked extensively with treating juvenile delinquents through dietary management.

Reed put her patients on a more natural, low-sugar diet to see if it made any difference in their behavior. After a few years on the program, those who were conscientiously following this diet had only one-sixth the incidence of repeat criminal offenses. Similar studies have produced like findings. The relationship between childhood hyperactivity and juvenile delinquency is confirmed again and again.

Circle of Influence Discussion

It is very important that you have a discussion with individuals that have impact on your children:

☑ Teachers   ☑ Grandparents

☑ Day care employees   ☑ Family members

☑ Church members   ☑ Neighbors

☑ Sunday school teachers   ☑ Coaches

You **must** discuss with everyone who has contact with your child about the importance of the new diet. It is your responsibility to have this discussion on a regular basis. Explain that you are making a monumental change in your family's lifestyle and they should respect your decision. Trust yourself. Be confident that you know what is best for your family.

I can recall on occasion when my parents watched my oldest son when he was very young. Upon my arrival home they were very excited and proud to tell me that they had given him cranberry juice. This is the one and only time in my son's nearly twenty years that he was totally not himself. Whatever was in that juice made him an unrecognizable child because he had absolutely no control, I could see how chemicals affected him. These chemicals alter fat metabolism and neuro-transmitters (chemical sending messages). If children are continually consuming these chemicals, it is frightening to think about what is happening to their nervous systems.

What About Birthdays?

Eating sugar-laced foods at birthday parties and other celebrations depletes the body and alters the metabolism.

Eating sugar-laced foods at birthday parties and other celebrations depletes the body and alters the metabolism. It is going to be your decision to follow through in making appropriate cakes and cookies for your child to consume (i.e., no sugar, using the sugar alternative suggestions). **You can find easy-to-make cake mixes with great ingredients at any health food store.**

Going Off Medication

I'm not in a position to tell anybody who is reading this book to stop taking medication. This is a discussion that you will need to have with your health care provider. Often health care providers do not see any way but their own—which may be the continued use of medication. I would encourage you to monitor your child.

I have patients who independently decided to reduce the amount of medication when appropriate and made the necessary lifestyle changes. Holidays, vacations and summertime are excellent times to monitor your child and make changes. If you are making changes on your own, please notify your child's circle of influence.

Exercise & Social Activities

Physical exercise is a definite adjunct to our program. Exercise increases blood flow, which means more oxygen. Oxygen promotes life. Muscles require fuel. Fuel can be sourced from the glucose in the blood and fat. Regular exercise will keep your child's endorphins (feel good hormones) elevated. Exercise

Exercise improves self-image and self-confidence and helps one maintain focus.

improves self-image and self-confidence and helps one maintain focus. Any type of exercise is great—group, team or individual. The more activity, the better. Martial arts is an excellent exercise and focus activity.

Remember—when the exercise activity is over, don't fill up on trans fat french fries, soda, ice cream novelties, donuts and chips. Eat fresh snacks such as water, juice, fruits, veggies, nuts, healthy chips with good fats (oleic safflower, sunflower), etc.

Encourage activities where thinking is required. Plan family activities. Church youth groups, community and school group functions are great. Watch the snacks. Discuss the snack and eating plan before leaving the house. This avoids arguments, manipulation, negotiation, begging, whining and impulsive giving in to temptation.

Start a self-help group to discuss the ideas presented here. Work together. Talk to your local pediatrician, school administrators, health food stores and local natural care doctors. Self-support groups will give you **allies**. You will need allies to continue, especially if this information is new to you.

Sample letter to your circle of influence

Dear _____,

Our family has exciting news. We have a plan to reverse (patient's name) dependency on medication to control his/her Hyperactivity/ADD/ADHD/ODD. We are going to be making lifestyle changes, including our family's eating habits. We have discovered a book that describes in detail why (patient's name) has been challenged with Hyperactivity/ADD/ADHD/ODD. The book is written by an experienced natural health care provider. The information points out exactly what we need to do. The bottom line is to normalize fat metabolism. This is going to mean everyone that is a part of (patient's name) circle of influence will need to help us.

The program must be strongly supported for a minimum of three months. We have enclosed examples of information as to how we will need you to assist us. It really is going back to the way life used to be.

We want to thank you in advance for your help.

Sincerely,

The Family of (patient's name)

www.DrBob4Health.com
Click on "Stop the Hype."

Robert F. DeMaria, D.C., D.A.B.C.O.
362 E. Bridge Street
Elyria, Ohio 44035

Re:

To Whom It May Concern:

_____, has made a decision to make necessary and immediate lifestyle changes to improve their overall state of health. I am requesting that you make a note in their file that they are not to consume dairy products, including cow's milk, yogurt, ice cream, cheese, cottage cheese or any other milk product that would come from a cow.

Research reveals that the consumption of dairy products may, in fact, precipitate unnecessary health and behavioral challenges in many children.

Thank you in advance for supporting this request.

Sincerely,

Robert F. DeMaria, D.C.

Teacher/Day Care Daily Guide

Teacher: Are you frequently faced with behavioral problems in your classroom? Is it disrupting the educational process? Do you find families resistive to using medications or do you find the medication protocol falling short of improving your student's performance? Did you know there is a more natural, more basic approach that has proven to be effective? It combines dietary changes and spinal subluxation maintenance care. This is a combined approach that works. It's not always easy—but no medication is needed. You can offer your families an alternative to medication and see improvement. You could implement the program right into your classroom.

We need your help. You spend a lot of time with our child. You are a key player in his/her inner circle of influence. Your support is vital and will impact this child's future in a very positive way. You will be very surprised once this child's metabolism is normalized. The key to this success is the normalization of fat metabolism.

☑ **She/he needs motivational comments.** Encourage the entire class not to consume hydrogenated or partially hydrogenated fats. Review the fat metabolism charts in the front of the book. Go over the charts with other families that may be having a problem or facing the challenge of hyperactivity.

☑ **We need positive comments about food modification.** You could possibly set up a rewards program in the classroom in which your students can have a diet free of sugar and hydrogenated fats for a certain period of time. It is very important that all the children have adequate minerals and understand food basics. The biggest obstacle that you may have to deal with is the media, advertising blitz of the fast food giants, the dairy association and the food pyramid.

☑ **Dairy foods plug up the lymphatic systems** and is the primary reason for ear infections and acne in teenagers. I would encourage you to read Dr. Oski's book, *Don't*

Drink Your Milk. This easy-to-read text is now utilized in institutions that train teachers.

☑ **Encourage parents to make positive changes.** Work with the child. Get a calendar and keep track of changes. Talk about preparing foods at home. Perhaps you could have a conversation with the parents about what the child likes, which could be used as part of a rewards system. Please be a positive encouragement. Send an encouraging note home with the child. If this child is currently taking Ritalin/Adderall, it could advance to Clonidine, Paxil and then Prozac. We need cooperation in your school, in your city, in your county, in your state and in our country. If not, we are going to continue the downward spiral. You alone can make a difference. We need your help.

☑ **Please talk with parents about the various menus that they are utilizing.** Please don't use sweets and candy containing sugar or high-fructose corn syrup as a reward in your classroom. Please look to the health food store for alternative ideas. We have great results with non-sugared, non-chemically altered food.

Patient's Guide

If necessary, read this to the patient in words they can understand.

Are you tired of being sick and tired? I'll bet you are! There's hope and there's help. It won't always be easy and you will have to be willing to help yourself. It would be a great benefit if you had a conversation with your family about your life and this program. Surprise everyone and join in on preparing food.

This book was written for you. Your family and friends will need your help. This is a guide to help your family and circle of friends help you get to the next level. They need your help.

☑ **Work on your posture.** Stand up straight and do the head glide exercises. Head glide exercises are very important along with the overall posture exercise. You will want to be checked by a natural health care provider that corrects posture and subluxation.

☑ **Regular exercise is beneficial.** I would encourage you to shut off the T.V.

☑ **Work on rewards with your family.** In other words, sit down and map out exactly what you want to do as far as preparing food, going grocery shopping with each other and talking about a type of reward for yourself. You need to work together.

☑ **Don't make a big deal about your lifestyle change.** If you are at a party or function and food that you shouldn't eat is served, find foods that are permissible. There is usually some type of veggie plate and/or protein (chicken, turkey, etc.) that can be consumed. Do not consume soda pop. Drink water. Request sparkling water that does not contain sugar.

☑ **Please help your entire family.** It will take a minimum of 102 days for your body to get on the road to health. Take your supplements, drink water and minimize consumption of dairy products and snack food fats (including french fries).

If you make these changes, I will guarantee there will be a positive response. The noise and commotion that goes on in your head will happily go away.

Go to DRBOB4HEALTH.COM and print out your own "Stop the Hype" certificate. Congratulations!!!

E-mail me your success story at DrBobIdidit@yahoo.com.

Notice

Excessive dairy consumption can interfere with fat metabolism. Milk on sugary cereal or consumed as a beverage and dairy confection (i.e., ice cream sandwiches and candy bars) is a part of the cause.

NOTES:

18
Prizewinning Pilot Program

Participants in our program included married couples, young children, teens, family members from solid homes, mixed homes, blended environments and single-parent families. Most experienced immediate improvement. A few had more of a struggle, but only two families that started the program did not finish. One young man was on stomach medication that his family felt prevented him from participating; a mom and her son, as they began participtation in the program, unexpectedly had to go out of state for personal reasons. My other participants did extremely well.

I needed participants for a project to help resolve ADD, ADHD, ODD and hyperactivity. I needed individuals that knew nothing about natural care. We screened all those who applied and only declined those who could not commit to the 102 days of lifestyle modification. I knew there would need to be alterations in lifestyle or there would be no change in behavior challenges.

All the participants began with the same pre-programmed ideas: the only treatment for the problem is medication. They were under the assumption that the food they were eating had nothing to do with their child's problem.

The pilot program is described below. The participants were at a disadvantage because they had no book to follow. They participated because they were tired of medicine and being forced into a corner by educators or school systems, physicians and peer pressure. At first, making changes was challenging, but the vast majority showed improvement within two weeks. This created excitement, enthusiasm and an overall sense of well-being.

We started with a meeting of our first wave of participants on a Saturday. My wife (and health training partner) and I began by presenting the rules for change. After the participants had followed the program for only 23 days—we were all ready to celebrate!

I. Lifestyle Pattern—REQUIRED

- Record Daily Dietary History—With Symptoms
- Dietary Modification—REQUIRED

   a. NO hydrogenated fats. Use prepared foods with high oleic safflower, high oleic sunflower, olive and coconut oils. French fries baked or cooked in approved oils. See page 98.

   b. NO cow's milk. Substitute with nut or grain milk. Breakfast with oatmeal, eggs, almond butter, bean burritos. Use imagination. Minimal refined carbohydrates.

   c. NO refined sugar. Use stevia, barley malt, brown rice syrup, Fruit Source™. Use juice sweetened spritzers vs. soda for a substitute beverage.

- Shop at local groceries with health food products and/or health food stores. Use what you have at home. Minimize the obvious. **Recipes can be found on my web page also.**

II. Exercise Regularly

- Walk, run, play basketball, swim, bike, jump rope, etc. Do some type of regular exercise three times weekly, 20 minutes minimum.

III. Supplementation (see product inquiry information)

- First Month

  - ➢ Take one salmon capsule per night (1) for the first 18 days

  - ➢ Take 1 tablespoon of flax oil per 100 lbs. daily or 12 capsules per 100 lbs.

  - ➢ Six Vitamin B daily, 2 at each meal (total of 6)

  - ➢ Three Vitamin B6 daily, 1 at each meal (total of 3)

  - ➢ Three mineral tablets daily, 1 at each meal (total of 3).

- Second Month and Continued

  - ➢ Daily take 1 tablespoon flax/12 capsules per 100 lbs.

  - ➢ Three Vitamin B daily (3)

  - ➢ One mineral tablet daily (1)

  - ➢ One Vitamin B6 daily (1)

- Diet Duration

  - ➢ **Take one salmon capsule at night when hydrogenated fats, dairy or refined sugar is consumed.**

There are dozens of dietary supplement companies; some are better than others. The products can be easily obtained at most health food stores or natural health care providers. The cost for the first month of the program was about $45; the second month less than $40. For only a small investment they found tremendous improvement and relief from symptoms. You too can make a big impact on your child. This investment will pay for itself the first month.

I would like to categorize the information gleaned from various participants to help you better make the appropriate changes in your family's life. The major modifications you make at first will seem overwhelming. **Most people do not**

want to change, yet they expect different results. This is very common in all patients I see. Core beliefs about the benefit of medicine have been so engrained in our consciousness that it requires a book, with this information, to educate you, the consumer, why you need to change.

Participant History

Most of the participants in our pilot program saw positive results in less than 23 days. By far the biggest complaint I got from the children was, "I am not going to eat that health food." They soon found out that health food tastes good and what they had been eating was a compression of devitalized food pieces. The parents learned that they had to participate in their children's eating choices.

The medication most of the participants had been utilizing included Ritalin, Effexor, Adderall, Prozac, Neurontin and Dexadrine. Parents had been spending anywhere from $100-$500 per month in prescription costs. We also had individuals who took no medication, but were in the process of needing to make a choice for treatment.

The family doctor, school psychologist, clinical psychiatrist or pediatrician normally made the health diagnosis for the patient. The diagnosis was made from various testing procedures, including interviews, screenings, questionnaires and teacher analysis. Some participants had more than one interview.

Helping Kids Eat Right

Healthier eating habits will decrease cravings for sugar and junk food, enhance your child's nutritional profile, and prevent obesity.

"The Healing Grocery
When Food Is Your Best Midicine"
By Kate Chynoweth
Alternative Medicine
September 2002

Symptoms prior to starting the program:

☑ Tiredness
☑ Lack of alertness
☑ Extreme distraction
☑ Poor posture
☑ Depressed appearance
☑ Mad facial expressions
☑ Depression
☑ Weepiness
☑ Rage
☑ Restlessness
☑ Low self esteem
☑ Difficulty focusing
☑ Inability to complete school work
☑ Difficulty socializing
☑ Fearful of change
☑ Did not like being alone
☑ Excessive crying

☑ Poor attention span
☑ Fearful
☑ Constant frustration
☑ Sulkiness
☑ Fidgety
☑ Whininess
☑ Gives up easily
☑ Dark circles under the eyes
☑ Moodiness
☑ Impulsivity
☑ Lack of concentration
☑ Short attention span
☑ Does not like the word 'no'
☑ Can't keep still
☑ Must be doing something
☑ Talkativeness
☑ Daydreaming state

The presenting body signals of participants included: ADD, depression, bipolar, ADHD, ODD, hyperactivity, food allergies, dyslexia, asthma, dysthymic disorder, extreme headaches, loss of appetite, depression (constant), severe mood swings, crying, looks drugged, feels better, a lot of ups and downs, nervous reactions, pick and chew fingers and nails, constipation and red eyes.

The behavioral challenges prevented patients from making friends, limited school success, affected focus and follow-through. They could not try new things alone, always seemed to be blamed for something and many times had low self-esteem. Concentration and completion of tasks was difficult. They could not sit still and had difficulty studying. There was less family harmony—the family could not eat out or were limited when shopping. Patients had a difficult time getting up for school and had difficulty with reading and comprehension.

There was no specific pattern in children of natural child-birth or c-section, and no specific childbirth complications requiring forceps. The biological family relationships of the participants are interesting. There were adopted children and single parents. The adopted children had a common history of abuse and neglect and the biological mother's history was unknown.

Most families ate out two to three times weekly. Breakfast was eaten at home; lunch was eaten out. Two to three bags of french fries were consumed weekly. The general consensus as to cause was a direct link to diet. Yet, no one mentioned hydrogenated fats, dairy and sugar as the most common foods leading to the problem. Parental background was varied with one participant suggesting a parent as a source of the challenge, i.e. on drugs or alcohol. A busy lifestyle also appeared as a possible factor.

Feedback After the First Month

Positive results from the first three weeks on the program included:

☑ Feeling really good physically and emotionally

☑ Going to the bathroom more

☑ Weight loss

☑ Sugar craving subsided

☑ Attention improving

☑ Teachers noticed change

☑ Decreased whining

☑ Tasks now being completed

☑ Overall health improved

☑ No morning vomiting

☑ Fewer stomachaches

☑ Fewer headaches

☑ Less complaint of bones hurting

☑ Reduced cramping

☑ Feels healthy

☑ Enjoys the new food

☑ Feels calmer

☑ Less argumentative

☑ Fewer struggles with daily routine

☑ More energy

☑ More ability to do exercise

☑ Skin improving (psoriasis going away)

☑ No menstrual cramping

☑ No constipation

☑ Not picking fingers

☑ Can concentrate at school

☑ Faster, better reader

☑ Memory improvement

☑ Improved concentration

☑ More stabilized

The biggest challenges the first month included:

- ☑ Taking the flax
- ☑ Taking time to exercise
- ☑ Understanding the connection between subluxation and diet
- ☑ Taking the pills
- ☑ Sweet tooth
- ☑ Getting use to new food
- ☑ Not being able to eat "regular food"
- ☑ Misses macaroni and cheese
- ☑ The food
- ☑ Avoiding sugar
- ☑ Finding alternatives
- ☑ Avoiding fast food
- ☑ Moods and focus
- ☑ Cutting down on caffeine
- ☑ Focusing
- ☑ Cost variety
- ☑ Missing junk food
- ☑ Pizza
- ☑ "Little Debbies"
- ☑ Misses soda pop
- ☑ Chocolate Milk
- ☑ Cookies
- ☑ "Hoho's"
- ☑ "Twinkies"
- ☑ Cappuccino
- ☑ Orange pop
- ☑ Fried cheese
- ☑ Suckers and gum

Comments and Advice Shared by Participants

☑ Drink lots of water with the program, especially with the salmon capsules.

☑ Follow the directions and you might lose weight. You will feel better and laugh more.

☑ Prepare yourself for different tasting foods.

☑ You do this to be healthy, it's good for your body, overall health improvement, better self-esteem. You must have discipline.

☑ We are starting to focus as a family.

☑ The food modifying is difficult at first, but each week it gets a little easier.

☑ The change came after a few weeks and it is noticeable.

☑ I see my whole family is better, sleeps better. Be patient with yourself and child. Reading labels is a must.

☑ I feel a lot better. I am sleeping better. Although you have good and bad days, eventually you'll feel great.

☑ Increase minerals if your child has trouble sleeping, experiences stress challenges or mood swings.

☑ Increase flax if your child has increased moments of crying* or increased itching.

(*We did discover that about five to six weeks into the lifestyle change some participants had a tendency to cry without reason. This heralds the need for Vitamin B. You may need to increase the whole food B complex.)

Feedback After the Second Month

☑ Therapist noticed child is calmer

☑ Meals and food shopping is easier

☑ Does not crave sugar

☑ Better grades, socializing better, more self-control

☑ Not whining or depressed, more energy

☑ Likes healthy alternatives

☑ Lost weight and warts are gone

☑ Teacher thinks he is still on Ritalin

☑ Happier with himself

☑ Adapted to the change

☑ Less colds

☑ Family environment more happy; enjoy talking about food and eating habits

☑ Better grades; more focused

☑ Easier to get along with

☑ Pays attention better

☑ Not as sick

☑ 100% improvement in health

☑ Not craving dairy

☑ More energy; less depressed

☑ Classmates are supportive

☑ Talking about food and how it makes them feel

☑ Sleeps better

☑ More tolerant of people and confrontation

☑ Fewer sore throats, headaches, and episodes of fatigue

☑ Asthma and bronchitis are better; not been on antibiotics since program began

☑ More energy, better concentration at school

☑ Stopped itching

☑ Going to the bathroom more

☑ Not vomiting every day

The biggest challenges after two months

- ☑ Being at parties and unable to eat the same food as the other kids
- ☑ Getting used to flax
- ☑ Diet change takes time to plan
- ☑ Difficulty with focusing
- ☑ Not having support of teachers
- ☑ Craves chocolate during period
- ☑ Craves sugar
- ☑ Teacher sees no change in school

The participants needed to make dietary and lifestyle changes to be successful with the program. All were motivated, but did not want to be deprived of food. The families increased communication about food choices; shopping together resulted in an improved family environment. Participants learned about various food items, especially snacks. There was immediate elimination of the improper food groups, especially milk and sweets.

One of the bigger challenges was careful shopping, making right food choices, being aware of the budget and choosing the right foods to pack for "day trips" and school.

Common challenges included dietary choices on holidays, at parties and school activities. Most participants were aware of these situations and brought appropriate foods for the occasion. Most teachers were supportive.

Students generally improved in school, manifested in better grades, improved self-esteem, reading and behavior. The overall result with all participants was very positive. The participant's emotional lives improved. Improved behavior was linked to lifestyle modifications and the elimination of unhealthy foods.

The pain of hyperactivity, ADD and ADHD appears to be stronger than the pleasure of the "forbidden foods"!

Feedback After the Third Month

The participants adapted solidly to the program by the third month. Motivation was fueled by the improvement in behavior and a general state of improved health.

When asked, "What can you tell others starting the program," the participants overwhelmingly responded with, "it is worth the challenge and it gets easier." The participants generally bought school lunches prior to the program; once the program started they began packing lunches. They all ate breakfast at home prior to the program and continued this throughout. **Lesson Learned:** *You need to control what you eat by preparing your own food*.

There was a mix of participants: those discontinuing medication, others not taking any medication, and those more intense cases who were still on medication. Subluxation correction was used as a part of our pilot program. The participants welcomed and enjoyed the "relief" of built-up tension and the over all health benefits associated with their spinal adjustments. **Lesson #2:** *Spinal adjustment can relieve tension build-up.*

Our participants completed the program with overwhelming success. We were one person shy of unanimity to continue with the lifestyle changes. The most common response was to stick with the supplements and flax and to stay away from hydrogenated fats and sugar. The pleasure of being calm has been a very motivating factor. **Lesson #3:** *Stay away from hydrogenated fats and sugars.*

Circles of influence noticed behavioral improvement. The consensus by the participants included better focus and improved schoolwork. Less discipline was required to maintain order. Our youngest participant was able to go on the bus without being carried on. He could also go shopping without being strapped to the cart. Schoolwork improved with great significance, grades going from "F" to "C." Testing and focus improved generally.

Using flax oil appeared to be a leading factor for the improvement as did the elimination of sugar, dairy and hydrogenated fats. **Lesson #4:** *Taking flax oil is a leading factor in health improvement.*

Much to everyone's surprise, the flu and cold season passed over all the participants. Our clinic patients have strong immune systems and rarely have body signals that are correlated with sickness. One young man was very excited because he did not get pneumonia, which has been a part of his life since childhood. He was able to participate in winter sports and ski for the first time. He was also able to discontinue six medications, including three inhalers, Neurontin, Prozac, Clonidine, Dexadrine and antibiotics.

The hardest obstacle during the program was making the diet changes, including eliminating sugar.

A challenge, especially for blended or divorced families, was convincing the other parent to support the lifestyle changes.

Common accomplishments reported by participants included making better grades, getting along with others, increased knowledge of food and the feeling of controlling their own destiny. One participant said he was having fun, which he had never had before. The participants were more aware of what goes on with the body, and they learned taking flax oil helps.

The concluding thoughts about the program are very positive. I knew, even before I started putting the information in written form and in a logical format, the program physiologically had to work. My patients and their parents have been educated to eat quality, physiologically-correct foods and supplements. They understood the role of spinal subluxations. The parents now do not have hyperactive or ADD children. Before beginning the program the participants knew little or nothing about natural health care. Now they make decisions based on their diet changes and are following a plan.

But most importantly, the families were working together toward a goal. The program, apart from allowing these families to learn together, created a new bond within the family unit. Not only was there an increased awareness of health but an elevated awareness of each other.

The final chapter of this life-changing program is a tribute to the group of individuals who participated in it "to get better without drugs."

My participants are just like you. Your situations may be similar or different, but anyone can work to create a happy and healthy environment. **Your family can experience the same exhilaration by taking steps to achieve a Ritalin-free life.** No more dependency on drugs. Sickness will go away. Your family life will return to one of peace and quiet. Life will be good again. One mom put it so succinctly, "We decided to choose life."

Positive Experiences From My Practice

My name is Kyle L. and I'm 15 years old. I enjoy music, swimming, dancing and sports. I was diagnosed with ADHD. Then, four years later, I was diagnosed with Tourettes Syndrome. Although neither disorder interfered with my hobbies, I had a difficult time in school. My "tics" and impulsiveness got me into major trouble with the law and I was kicked out of school.

As a result of a newspaper article, three neurologists and five psychologists later, Dr. DeMaria contacted my parents. They were skeptical at first but agreed to meet with Dr. Bob.

After a series of X-rays, tests on my spine and blood work, Dr. Bob concluded that by changing my diet and lifestyle and receiving regular spinal adjustments

I could get better, not perfect or cured, but definitely better. He was right! My mom says my behavior is much better, but I've still got a long way to go. My attitude has improved. By sticking to my diet and exercise plan, I can avoid a lot of problems.

I strongly encourage you to. . . TRY DR. BOB! IT REALLY DOES WORK!!

~

My mom brought me to Dr. DeMaria because we were dealing with A.D.D.—hyperactivity and impulsive behavior. After attending health meetings and hearing Dr. Bob on the radio, she decided to give his plan a try.

I had been taking 1¼ pills of Adderal a day and sometimes my appetite would diminish. My sleep was also affected. With Dr. Bob's prescription for a proper diet and nutritional supplements, I am now taking only ¼ pill a day. My attention span, appetite and sleep habits have improved. For the first time I said, "Mom, I'm tired"—I actually wanted to go to bed. My penmanship skills and small muscle skills have also improved.

Dr. Bob and his staff are very helpful and friendly. My mom loves the results we are getting. We have also learned so much about my health and how to improve my diet for best results with A.D.D.

~

I have a patient who has a son living with his mother. This individual also has two daughters from his second marriage. I have treated both daughters beginning early in their life. The two young girls do not consume hydrogenated fats; they watch their diet. There is no hyperactivity, ADD or ADHD symptoms.

On the other hand, the son, who lives with his mother, has been allowed to consume whatever he wanted. This resulted in very many neurologic challenges including twitching and altered hand and body movements. The young man was on the verge of being placed on Ritalin when the dad spoke to me about what was going on with his son. I advised him to make the changes discussed in this book, especially the elimination of hydrogenated fats.

Within a very short time period (three months) this young man's twitching disappeared.

≈

I have a young boy who is about ten years old who was having repeated hand motions, facial movement and challenges with schooling. After adding minerals and Flax oil to his diet, in conjunction with spinal adjustments, his twitches and excessive activity disappeared.

≈

Tina is a 68-year old female who presented with a history of three spinal surgeries, hysterectomy, gall bladder removal, lumpectomy and sinus surgery. She was very keyed-up and failed to calm. We placed her on minerals and flax oil. Within one week, in conjunction with her spinal adjustments, her symptoms subsided.

19

Hype-Free Irresistible Recipes

The following recipes can very be made at home very easily and used as a substitute for commercially-prepared foods. These recipes do not include ingredients that contribute to hyperactivity but rather offers alternatives that maintain a healthy body and sharp mind.

I have been advising my patients to limit soy products to eight ounces daily. All the long-term effects of modern soy are not known yet.

As a family, explore these new foods. Enjoy their diverse flavors and have fun with growing healthy together!

These ingredients can be found in most health food stores and in the health food section of progressive grocery stores. You can use the web page contact listed in the book for direct sources of foods.

A manual spray pump for oil, including olive, high oleic safflower or sunflower as an oil source is a recommendation to coat cooking pans and dishes.

MIGHTY MEALS

Easy Chicken and Rice
1 can (15 ounces) clear chicken broth
3/4 cup water
1 cup brown rice, uncooked
4 boneless chicken breasts, skinned
1 small onion, chopped
1 tablespoon (Tbls.) dried parsley
1/2 teaspoon (tsp.) celtic sea salt
1/4 tsp. black pepper
1/2 tsp. garlic powder
1 tsp. tarragon
1 bag (16 ounces) mixed vegetables,
    frozen or fresh

Preheat oven to 350°. Pour chicken broth and water in a large roasting pan. Add brown rice. Top with chicken breasts. Sprinkle with onion, parsley, salt, pepper, garlic powder and tarragon.

Cover roasting pan with lid. Bake for 1 1/2 hours. Adding the vegetables during the last 30 minutes of cooking. Makes 4 servings.

Broccoli-Cheese Frittata
3 eggs
3 Tbls. nut milk
1/4 tsp. celtic sea salt
Dash of cayenne pepper
2 tsp. olive oil
10 ounces chopped broccoli
1 small onion, finely chopped
1 small clove garlic, crushed
2 cups rice or soy cheddar cheese, shredded

Combine eggs, milk, salt and red pepper; beat well and set aside.

Heat oil in a 10-inch skillet. Add broccoli, onion and garlic; sauté until tender. Remove from heat. Stir in egg mixture. Sprinkle with shredded cheese.

Cover and cook over low heat for 10 minutes or until egg is set and cheese is melted.

Cut into 4 wedges and serve immediately. (Makes 4 servings)

Enchilada Bake
2 Tbls. olive oil
1/2 cup minced scallion
2 Tbls. whole-wheat flour
1 cup vegetable stock
2 cups cooked or canned pinto beans, drained
3/4 tsp. celtic sea salt
12 soft corn tortillas
2 cups chunky salsa
1 1/2 cups firm silken tofu, drained
1 4-ounce can diced green chilies
2 Tbls. lime juice
1/2 cup grated soy Cheddar cheese

Preheat the oven to 350°. Heat the oil in a medium skillet over medium heat. Add the scallion and cook for about 3 minutes or until softened. Stir in the flour and cook 1 minute. Add the stock and cook, stirring to achieve a smooth consistency about 1 minute longer. Add the pinto beans and 1/2 tsp. of the salt and set aside.

Lightly oil a baking dish or coat with nonstick cooking spray. Line the bottom of the dish with a layer of 4 tortillas. Spread with half of the salsa and cover with half of the pinto bean mixture. Repeat the layers, ending with a layer of 4 tortillas and set aside.

In a small bowl, combine the tofu with the chilies and limejuice and remaining 1/4 tsp. salt, whisking until smooth. Pour over the layered bean and tortilla mixture.

Cover and bake for 25 minutes. Remove the cover; top with the soy cheese. Bake, uncovered, 5 to 10 minutes longer to melt the cheese. (Makes 8 servings.)

Italian Swiss Steak
1 pound lean round steak, trimmed of all fat
1/2 cup water
1 medium onion, thinly sliced
1 green pepper, thinly sliced
2 small tomatoes, cut into wedges
1/4 pound fresh mushrooms
1/2 tsp. dried basil
1/2 tsp. dried oregano
1 Tbls. dried parsley
1/2 tsp. garlic powder
1/2 tsp. celtic sea salt
1/2 tsp. black pepper
2 cups whole wheat pasta noodles,
    cooked and hot

Preheat oven to 350°. Brown steak in a nonstick skillet; add water.

Place steak and water in a roasting pan. Top with onion, green pepper, tomatoes and mushrooms. Sprinkle basil, oregano, parsley, salt and pepper over the top.

Cover and bake for 1 1/2 hours. Serve over whole-wheat pasta noodles. (Makes 4 servings)

Macaroni and Cheese

The ultimate comfort food—without dairy products. A perfect meal for a blustery evening or "just because." Serve with stewed tomatoes for a real trip down memory lane.

2 Tbls. olive oil
1/2 cup minced onion
2 Tbls. whole-wheat flour

2 cups warmed nut/rice milk
1/2 tsp. celtic sea salt
1/8 tsp. freshly ground pepper
1/8 tsp. ground nutmeg
1 pound pasta elbows, cooked and drained
2 cups grated soy Cheddar cheese

Preheat oven to 375°. Heat the oil in a saucepan over medium heat, add the onion and cook 5 minutes. Stir in the flour and cook for 2 minutes, then reduce the heat to very low and slowly whisk in the hot nut/rice milk. Continue to cook, stirring for about 3 minutes or until the mixture thickens. Season with salt, pepper, and nutmeg.

Combine the sauce with the cooked pasta and a cup of soy cheese. Spoon into a baking dish and top with the remaining 1 cup rice/nut cheese.

Bake for 30 to 40 minutes or until heated through. (Makes 4 servings.)

Marvelous Meatloaf
2 pounds ground round
(you may substitutes ground turkey)
2 cups old-fashioned oats, uncooked
3/4 cups onion, minced
1/4 green pepper, minced
2 eggs, slightly beaten
1/2 tsp. celtic sea salt
1/2 tsp. black pepper
1 Tbls. Worcestershire sauce
1 tsp. dry mustard
1/4 cup nut/rice milk
3/4 cup tomato sauce

Preheat oven to 400°. In a large bowl, combine all ingredients, except 1/2 cup tomato sauce; mix well.

Shape meat into 2 loaves and place on rack to allow fat to drain. Spread half of remaining tomato sauce on top of each loaf.

Bake for 40 minutes. Makes 8 servings.

Dairyless Alfredo Sauce
1/2 cup blanched almonds
1/2 cup water
1/2 cup soymilk
1 minced shallot
2 cloves minced garlic
1 Tbls. olive oil
Dash nutmeg
Salt, white pepper to taste

To make:
In blender or food processor, puree almonds, water and milk until smooth. In sauté pan, cook shallot and garlic in oil on low heat until soft, about 3 minutes. Do not brown. Add almond mixture; simmer until sauce thickens, about 3 to 4 minutes. Add nutmeg, salt and pepper. Makes about 1 cup or enough sauce for 4 servings of pasta.

Herbed Veggie Gravy
1/3 cup whole wheat pastry flour
1 cup rice milk
1 Tbls. soy sauce
1 cup water
2 Tbls. olive oil
1 tsp. dried, crushed sage
1/4 tsp. thyme
1/4 tsp. marjoram
Salt and pepper to taste

To make:
In a 2 quart saucepan, heat oil over medium heat. Add flour, and stir often for 2 minutes. Remove from heat and allow to cool.

Combine all remaining ingredients in a bowl. Whisk together with the flour/oil, half at a time to avoid lumping. Bring to a boil over medium heat, stirring often. Reduce heat to low and cool for 10 minutes. Adjust seasonings, add water to thin consistency. Stores well in refrigerator for several days.

Vegetable Chowder
1 Tbls. olive oil
1 small diced onion stalk
1 large celery stalk
1 large carrot, thinly sliced
1 clove garlic, finely diced
1 medium Russet potato, peeled and diced
2 ripe tomatoes, chopped
1/2 cup fresh or frozen corn
2 Tbls. tamari or soy sauce
2 cups rice milk
1 large bay leaf
Salt/Pepper
2 cups water
1 tsp. basil

To make:
Saute onions and olive oil in saucepan on medium heat. Add celery, carrots and garlic and sauté for 5 minutes. Add water, potatoes, corn and seasonings. Bring to a boil and then reduce heat to simmer.

Cover and cook for 15 minutes. Add tomatoes and simmer 15 more minutes. Add rice milk. Adjust seasonings. Serves 6

Corn Bread
3/4 cup cornmeal
1/4 cup whole wheat pastry flour
1/4 cup unbleached flour
1 Tbls. baking powder
1/4 tsp. sea salt
1 beaten egg
1 cup rice milk

1/3 cup maple syrup
cinnamon sprinkles

To make:
Preheat oven to 375°F. Mix all dry ingredients in one bowl. Mix all wet ingredients in another bowl.

Stir wet ingredients into dry ingredients. Oil muffin tin and spoon in batter (2/3 full).

Bake for 20-25 minutes, until golden brown. Makes 12 muffins

Zesty Cornmeal Muffins
3/4 cup all purpose flour
1/4 cup flour (of choice)
1 cup yellow cornmeal
1/4 cup honey
4 tsp. baking powder
1tsp. salt
1 tsp. chili powder
1 cup nut (almond, rice, oat) milk
1/4 cup olive oil
2 eggs slightly beaten
3/4 cup shredded cheddar flavored rice/soy cheese
1/4 cup chopped green chilies
1/4 cup chopped jalapeno peppers

Preheat oven to 425°F. Coat muffin pan with vegetable cooking spray. In medium bowl, combine flours, cornmeal, honey, baking powder, salt and chili powder. In a separate bowl, stir together nut milk, oil and eggs. Add dry ingredients and blend slightly. Stir in cheese and peppers. Pour into muffin pan. Bake 18-24 minutes or until toothpick in center comes out clean. Remove muffins from pan and cool on wire rack.

DRESSINGS

Salad Dressing Supremo
3/4 cup Omega Flax oil or olive oil
1/4 cup balsamic vinegar
1tsp. Dijon mustard
2-4 cloves crushed garlic
1 tsp. Worcestershire Sauce
6 drops Tabasco sauce
1 Tbls. sweet basil
1/2 tsp. tarragon
1/2 tsp. oregano
1/4 cup rice milk parmesan cheese
1/2 tsp. maple syrup
1 Tbls. sun dried tomatoes (chopped)

Blend in blender or food processor. Store left over dressing in the fridge.

Herb Salad Dressing
Rich, pungent taste. Makes 2 ¼ cups
Preparation time: 5 minutes

Blend in blender:
   1 1/4 cups olive oil
   1/3-1/2 cup apple cider vinegar
   1/4 cup lemon juice
   1 Tbls. tamari
   1 tsp. garlic powder
   1/2 tsp. oregano
   1/4 tsp. marjoram
   1/4 tsp. tarragon
   1/4 tsp. rosemary
   2 Tbls. finely grated
      rice milk Parmesan cheese
   1/4 cup roasted sesame seeds, lightly toasted*
   1/2 tsp. dry mustard
      (optional—for a sharper taste)

To toast sesame seeds: Place a skillet over medium heat. Add sesame seeds. Stir frequently for several minutes until seeds begin popping and turn slightly darker in color. Be careful as they burn quickly.

Creamy Italian Dressing
Preparation time: 5-8 minutes—Makes 2 cups

Blend in blender:
> 1/3 cup water
> 1/4 cup apple cider vinegar
> 1 Tbls. honey
> 1 egg
> 1/2 tsp. celery seed
> 1/8 tsp. dry mustard
> 1 large clove garlic
> 1 tsp. savory
> 1 tsp. tarragon
> 1 tsp. salt
> 1/2 tsp. black pepper

While blender is on, slowly add: 1 cup olive oil

Green Goddess Salad Dressing
1 med. green onion (scallion)
1 med. clove of garlic
4 springs of parsley
3/4 tsp. sea salt
1 cup rice milk
3 Tbls. tahini

To make:
Combine all ingredients in a blender or food processor. Blend until smooth. 6 servings

SWEET SUGGESTIONS

Dreamy Soy Smoothie

1 frozen banana
2 large frozen strawberries
1 cups soy milk
1/2 cup orange juice, optional
ice cubes, optional

To make:
Place all ingredients in a blender and blend to combine.

Other ideas:
Take out the strawberries and add raw carob powder.
Pineapple, raspberries, blueberries, kiwi, etc.
Soy yogurt.

Apple Crisp—This is very good

2 cups cored sliced and pared baking apples
1/2 cup honey
1/4 cup whole wheat pastry flour
1/4 cup rolled oats
1/2 tsp. cinnamon
1/2 tsp. nutmeg
3 Tbls. soft butter

Heat oven to 350°. Place apples in greased loaf pan. Blend remaining ingredients until crumbly. Spread flour mixture over apples. Bake 30-35 minutes until the apples are tender and topping is golden brown. Serve warm.

Drop Sweet Cookies

Soft, chewy and delicately sweet, the secret of these is simplicity.

4 ounces soft tofu
1/2 cup brown rice syrup or honey
3 Tbls. olive or safflower oil
1 1/2 tsp. vanilla extract
1 cup whole wheat or unbleached pastry flour

1/2 tsp. each: baking powder, baking soda and salt
3/4 tsp. ground nutmeg
54 whole almonds (optional)

Preheat oven to 350°. In a blender, combine tofu, rice syrup, oil and vanilla until smooth. Set aside.

Sift together dry ingredients. Stir in tofu mixture and stir to combine. Drop by teaspoonfuls onto ungreased baking sheets. Top with almonds.

Bake for 7 minutes or until cookies are still puffy and have just begun to brown on the bottom.

Chocolate Chip Cookies
2 cups Organic Flour—You can use 1/2 whole
   wheat and 1/2 unbleached white—experiment
   with your own likings.
3/4 tsp. baking soda
3/4 tsp. sea salt (we use Celtic Sea Salt)
1 cup of softened butter (no margarine—just butter)
1 cup of Pear Sweet (from Wax Orchards—see our
   website link)
1 egg
1 tsp. vanilla
1 1/4 cup of malt sweetened chocolate chips
   (we use Sunspire brand)
Preheat oven to 350°

Combine dry ingredients and set aside. Beat butter and Pear Sweet until blended. Add egg and vanilla and blend these all with the dry ingredients. Add chips. Drop by spoonfuls onto ungreased cookie sheet. Bake for 10 minutes or until browned. You will get different amounts of cookies based on the type of flour you use and how big your spoonfuls are.

Extraordinary Pumpkin Bread

Here is a quick bread that really delivers. It will be the star at any gathering.

1 1/3 cup whole-wheat flour
　　(start with one then add ½ of the 1/3 cup)
1 tsp. baking soda
1 tsp. baking powder
1/2 tsp. cinnamon
Pinch of ground cloves
1/4 tsp. nutmeg
1/4 tsp. celtic sea salt
1/2 cup prune puree
1/2 cup pumpkin puree
1 cup granulated Fruitsource®
　　(or natural sweetener)
1 or 2 egg whites
1/4 cup cold water
1/2 cup vanilla rice milk
1/2 cup date nuggets or
　　chopped dates

Preheat oven to 350°. Lightly pump spray (spray with olive, safflower, or sunflower oil) a loaf pan

Sift first 7 ingredients into a medium-size bowl. Set aside.

Cream prune and pumpkin purees in a large bowl. Blend in Fruitsource®. Set aside.

Whisk egg whites with water until foamy and whisk into pumpkin mixture.

Add dry ingredients to liquid ingredients alternately with rice milk, mixing until just moistened. Fold in dates.

Pour into pan and bake about 50 minutes until golden brown and a toothpick inserted in center comes out clean.

Cool in pan for 10 mins. Remove to wire rack to cool completely.

Banana Nut Bread

1/3 cup butter
4 mashed bananas
1/2 cup honey
1/4 cup raw wheat germ
2 beaten eggs
3/4 cup whole wheat flour
1/4 cup soy milk powder
2 tsp. baking powder
1/2 tsp. vanilla
1 Tbls. nutritional yeast
1/2 cup nut flour
1/2 cup chopped almonds

Preheat oven to 350°. Cream butter and honey. Add eggs and mashed bananas.

Combine dry ingredients and mix with banana mixture. Stir in vanilla and nuts.

Bake in a 9x5x3 inch loaf pan for about 1 hr. Check periodically. Avoid too much browning.

Appendices

REFERENCE SOURCES
Product Inquiry Information

Use any product that is low dosage, cold-processed, whole food.

Contact your local natural health care provider or local health food store for products, **or you can order from Dr. Bob at 1-888-922-5672. We can ship what you need.**

Carlson Labs can be found in most health food stores. **www.carlsonlabs.com**. Carlson Labs is a great source for **salmon oil**.

Omega Nutrition is an excellent source for liquid **flax seed oil**. They carry liquid flax oil in various flavors, such as butterscotch and chili-garlic. They also have the flax in capsules and blended omega 6/3 oils for long-term use. Omega Nutrition is found in most health food stores or **www.omeganutrion.com**.

The Grain & Salt Company provides the very finest in **Celtic Sea Salt**. I encourage all of my patients to utilize this *mineral rich* product. Since granulated is also available, I would also encourage you to obtain a porcelain grinder. This is the easiest way to utilize the Celtic Sea Salt crystals in a fresh state. We also order our roasted and/or raw **almonds** from the company direct. Although there is an initial membership fee, you will see that over the long-term this is an excellent product and will improve your family's entire state of mineral health (one of the major reasons that individuals today have challenges with many chronic and debilitating diseases). Call **1.800.TOP.SALT**

Interplexus is a quality source of **probiotics**. It is very important to use a product that works. We have successfully utilized their three-step program. Call **1.800.875.0511** or **Dr. Bob at 1-888-922-5672**.

Standard Process, has by far the very best quality, **whole food supplements** that I have used. There may be other products that you can use to substitute for the Standard Process products.

However, if you have been using supplements and you're not feeling 100 percent, then those supplements apparently are not the answer for you. Contact your local natural health care provider or go to **www.standrdprocess.com** for a practitioner in your area. **This company is the source of B-Vitamins, B-6 and Minitran (a mineral product derived from alfalfa and kelp) which I use in my practice. I also use their Zymex II for parasite control.**

Parasites/ Yeast Controlling Products: Agrisept, A citric seed extract supplement is useful for controlling yeast. Call 888-922-5672. Nutritionist Ann Louise Gittleman, Ph.D. has used the homeopathic Aqua Phase formulas for yeast elimination with great success for over ten years. As the author of *Guess What Came to Dinner: Parasites and Your Health*, she is a strong proponent of the Verma and Para line of natural parasite cleansers. Call 800-888-4353 or visit www.unikeyhealth.com for further information. There are several products for parasite removal. Ask your health food store manager or health care provider.

Food Sources

You can go directly to **www.DrBob4Health.com** and find a listing of Dr. Bob's favorite web sites.

www.WaxOrchards.com will link you to literally hundreds of web pages you will find useful for finding your food products.

www.bluediamondgrowers.com – Nut-Thins are light, crispy wafers made from natural California rice and rich, flavorful tree nuts. With a mild nutty flavor and delightfully different texture, Nut-Thins are a tasty snack right out of the box or a savory complement to cheeses and dips.

www.diamondorganics.com – Organic quality food delivered to your home.

www.ener-g.com – Ener-G Foods' products make it easier to prepare delicious meals for people with food allergies and food intolerances. Wheat-free and gluten- free breads, buns, rolls, English muffins, pizza shells, brownies, cookies, donuts and fruitcakes are vacuum- packed to ensure freshness without freezing. Wheat and gluten-free baking mixes and flours include rice flours, tapioca flour, potato flour, potato starch, bean flour, rice bran and rice polish. Milk alternatives include soy-based Soyquik (soy-milk powder) and Lacto.

www.missroben.com – Hundreds of kid-friendly, gluten-free, casein-free products. Toll-free technical and baking assistance. Free catalog available.

www.glutensolutions.com – Available brands such as Authentic Foods, Ener-G Foods, Gluten-Free Pantry, Legumes Plus, Nature's Highlights, Pamela's Products, Pastariso, Really Great Food Company, Sylvan Border Farm and adding many more!

www.pamelasproducts.com – Indulge yourself! Delectable and decadent cookies, biscotti, baking mixes and more!

www.holgrain.com – Setting the standard for wheat- free, gluten-free products since 1912. Crackers, chocolate brownie mix, pancake and waffle mix, brown rice and bread crumbs, etc.

www.ebfarm.com – Takes the labor out of salad prepar- ation by offering fresh salad greens—all organic, pre-washed and pre-packaged—in an impressive variety of combinations.

www.glutenfreegrocery.com – This site will take the hassle out of finding your favorite gluten-free foods. Choose from over 200 delicious products and have them delivered in one convenient package.

www.feingold.org – This site provides families with support, specific product information and tips on how to make avoiding every-day chemicals easier on the shopper, the cook and the chemically sensitive.

www.GlutenFreeMall.com – Your special diet super store!

www.heintzmanfarms.com – A source of flax products from South Dakota. Rick Heintzman, owner/grower.

www.healthfromthesun.com – An organic source of flax products from Canada.

Forc Food Coop 1.888.936.9648, Food Coop Warehouse.

Websites related to the history of vaccines, their effects, and where to explore other options:

www.homeopathic.org
www.cdc.gov/nip
www.909shot.com
www.vaers.org

Information regarding drug abuse and the National Institute on Drug Abuse.
www.drugabuse.gov

Additional Reading: Dr. West's newsletter "Health Alert" is an outstanding source for health information. You can subscribe to the newsletter, Call: **831.372.2103**.

Renew Your Life, by Brenda Watson, C.T., is an excellent, easy-to-read book on digestion and detoxification. Call: **800.830.4778**.

Nutritional Microscopy Sources

The following organization can assist you in having a personal nutritional microscopy completed at their location. They may assist you in finding someone that may be closer to your geographic location. If you have been treated everywhere and have seen no improvement, it would be to your advantage to check out nutritional microscopy—including the dry slides—to rule out parasitic infestation.

If your child is on any of the common medications including, Ritalin, Adderall, Clonidine, Paxil, Prozac, etc., ask yourself: Are you going to continue with the same old routine, or are you going to draw a line in the sand, take a stand for yourself and make the necessary changes? Nutritional microscopy is a must. I know this may seem a stretch for some of you. In fact, you may be challenged by your health care provider.

For a Nutritional Microscopy practitioner near you, contact American Biologics at (619) 429-8200.

Products for Parasite Control
Used by Ann Louise Gittleman, Ph.D.

The Verma and Para Systems consist of all natural ingredients of clinically tested, time-honored herbs and digestive aides which are designed to eliminate intestinal worms and parasites from the GI tract, blood, organs and tissues. Please visit www.unikeyhealth.com for more information about these products and to read the testimonials of satisfied users who have found relief from parasite-based symptoms such as persistent bloating, gas, food allergy, chronic fatigue, nervousness, skin problems, teeth grinding and reactive arthritis.

E.Y.I. Products Used by Dr. Bob

Agrisept-L®, Parablast®, Triomin®, IsoGreens® and Oxy-Up® are products from Essentially Yours. Agrisept-L® is for individuals who need to first normalize their chronic parasitic or yeast challenge in their body. We also use Parablast® when there is major parasite involvement. Triomin™ can be used as an ionic mineral, 1 ounce daily. I also encourage my patients to use Isogreens, which is a green food, 2 teaspoons is equivalent to 5 servings of organic fruits and vegetables. Because I believe that oxygen is deficient in our society today, I encourage Oxy-up® which is a stabilized liquid oxygen. Go to DrBob4Health.com and click on EYI Products, follow the directions.

Standard Process Product Information

Minitran	Cataplex B
✳ **Mineral used in program**	✳ **Whole Complex B Vitamin**
The combination of mineral complexes and nutrients in Mintran work together as a mild calmative, to establish balanced function of the central nervous system.	The complete vitamin B complex is composed of two primary divisions, Cataplex B and Cataplex G; each with complementary actions. Cataplex B contains different components of the B complex that are stimulatory to the metabolic, cardiovascular, and central and peripheral nervous systems.

The Elimination Program
Free Health Care

The elimination program is extremely powerful. And better yet, it is **free!** This therapy does just what its name implies: it allows you to eliminate offending foods in your diet that may trigger powerful disease syndromes: skin problems, migraine, severe muscle or joint pain and hyperactivity.

When asked to name the single most powerful therapy they know, the vast majority of holistic practitioners will say the elimination diet. I want to reinforce just how powerful this therapy can be.

The Elimination Diet is not easy, but is a way to determine if foods can be a part of your health problem. You may want to take flax oil and salmon oil three weeks prior to trying this. These oils are needed by the body to have strong healthy cell walls. The healthy cells result in strong intestine tissues. The Elimination diet may be difficult because the foods you crave the most could directly cause a health problem. Sometimes these foods cause a reaction in your body up to four days later.

There is a difference between allergy and sensitivity. Foods to which you are sensitive can result in joint pain, congestion and other symptoms which may send you to the physician. **Some of the most common problems caused by food allergies are digestive problems, skin problems, sinus congestion, pain syndromes, headaches and hyperactivity.** The Elimination Diet is a tool to see what foods may initiate negative symptoms.

Start With One Food

Step 1: Begin with a mono diet (one food only) for two to three days. For these initial days, the one food you are to eat is fresh, living food. The best choices are either fresh watermelon or fresh zucchini. (Watermelon or zucchini are best because they are among the least allergenic foods.)

The ideal season for the mono diet season is summer because watermelon and fresh zucchini are found in abundance. However, you can substitute another fresh, living food in any season, at any time of the year, and still expect similarly successful results. Do not skip this initial mono diet; the first days of one food only are the most critical part of the elimination program.

Stay on this mono diet for at least 48 hours and in some cases, up to 72 hours. At that time, the pain/syndrome you'd been experiencing can be expected to subside or disappear. If the pain/syndrome disappears when you are on the initial mono diet, it is proof positive that foods (of some type) are triggering the problem. This is **remarkably common**.

Finding the Culprits

You must stay on the mono diet until the syndrome subsides or disappears. If, after a week, **nothing changes**, you have ruled out foods as the trigger of your problems. However, if you feel better, your next job is to determine which of the foods you have eliminated are the triggers. And remember, it is best to inform your doctor of any fasting/ restrictive diet plans. It is also important to drink plenty of pure water during this period.

Step 2: Determine the trigger foods. Introduce other foods into your diet, one food at a time. It is this portion of the program that is more accurately called the elimination diet (with the initial phase of the program being the mono diet).

> **Flax oil works by giving cells necessary nutrients and building blocks to make healthy cell walls. Sickness and disease occurs at the cellular level. Though we look at hyperactivity as a major neurological breakdown, it is still cellular in origin. Scurvy is corrected by adding vitamin C, healing at the cellular level. We are living in exactly the same type of environment, today we have an Omega 3 fat deficiency in our society.**

The most common culprits are milk, wheat, pork, chocolate, and corn. But remember: *Any food can be a problem for you.* Even typically healthy foods.

When you eat an offending food, your body will tell you so by the return or worsening of symptoms within 24 hours. Once offending foods are discovered, most people need to eliminate them from their diet for a year or more. At that time, they can be tested again. Some patients may have deficiencies in other nutrients that allow the problem to continue. There is an excellent book called *The Ultimate Healing System*, by Dr. LePore. It is Dr. LePore's opinion that various nutritional deficiencies can often be the antidote for offending foods and food allergies. We have had success treating patients using this method.

Helping your child stick to the elimination diet will take love and patience. For the first few days, there may be a flare-up of hyperactivity due to withdrawal, and your youngster may rebel more than usual. It is very important that the elimination of allergic foods be followed very closely. Avoid a vicious circle: as the withdrawal of symptoms abate, the child eats a forbidden food, which sets off a reaction that starts him feeling bad all over again.

Rewards, comfort, praise, special treats and support are extremely important during the early stages. Encourage aerobic exercise five to six times a week. When the child starts feeling better as a result of the diet, friends and family start noticing the results. Because he no longer feels picked on, he will be more willing to stick to the regime without too much prodding.

While uncovering food allergies is an excellent way to start solving any health problems, foods may not be the root cause of the problem. For example, if pork caused migraines, then anyone who ate pork would get a migraine. This is not the case. Instead, pork is a trigger for migraines only in some people. And the same is true for all food allergies. The cause of the problem (why people are allergic to some foods) usually lies in the way each body reacts.

Nonetheless, discovering and eliminating the offending foods is powerful and common-sense therapy. You are wise to begin here. Would a couple years of antibiotics to clear up a skin condition make sense if you could eliminate the problem in days by eliminating a certain food out of your diet? Determining food allergies may save you from months or years of frustration with unsuccessful health care.

The Healthiest Diet In the World

The healthiest diet in the world is the Mediterranean diet. The Mediterranean-style diet is the most successful for the greatest number of people. I treat northern Europeans, Hispanics, Asians, African-Americans with the same basic formula. Hispanic's eat more rice and beans; Northern Europeans eat more meat and potatoes. I want the basic diet to be Mediterranean.

The American Food Pyramid is one that fast food restaurants use interspersed with highly processed foods. The Mediterranean diet is steeped in fruits, vegetables, beans, nuts, olive oil and more. I suggest this diet to my family and patients. People on this diet have fewer heart attacks and heart disease problems. Your child's present diet (hydrogenated fats and sugar) and hyperactive state will lead to an adult with heart disease. In time, children on the Mediterranean diet will have reduced hyperactivity and will be less likely to develop heart disease.

Scientists tracking the health benefits related to a diet concluded that all participants should be on the Mediterranean diet. After four years, those on the diet had two thirds fewer heart attacks and a third less hospitalizations for heart problems. Remarkably, (the cholesterol levels were about the same among those on the diet and those not, proving that cholesterol has little or nothing to do with heart attacks.) Recent reports and articles confirm that inflamed blood vessels rather than elevated cholesterol precipitate heart challenges. After taking gender, age, alcohol, lifestyle, etc. into account, it is obvious clinically that the Mediterranean diet is the most healthy diet. The co-author of the study sums it up: "Our trial confirms what we have known for many years—coronary heart disease is essentially a nutritional disease." I would like to add that, from my experience, the cause of hyperactivity, ADD and ADHD parallel coronary heart disease.

THIS is the pyramid that should be hanging in all doctor's office and school.

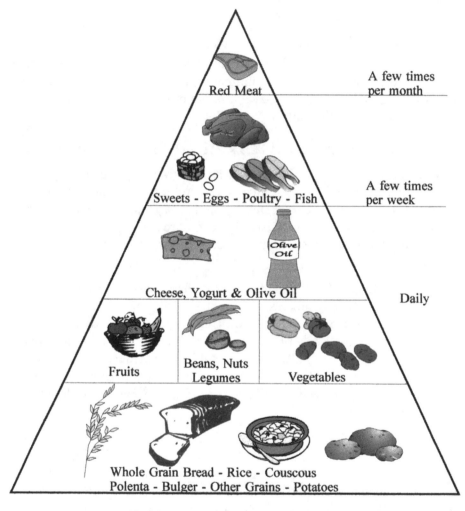

Mediterranean Food Pyramid

"Just Tell Me What To Do"
Simply Begin Here

WORKS CITED

A Better Life, *USA Today*, (January 6, 2003).

Braly, James. *Dr. Braly's Food Allergy & Nutrition Revolution*. New Canaan: Keats Publishing, 1992.

Budwig, Johanna. *Flax Oil as a True Aid Against Arthritis, Heart Infarction, Cancer and Other Diseases*. Vancouver: Apple Publishing Company, 1994.

Cook, William G. *Yeast Connection*. Tennessee: Professional Books, 1983.

Crowe, Sheila E. and Perdue, Mary H. "Gastrointestinal food hypersensitivity: Basic mechanisms of pathophysiology". *Gastroenterology*, Vol.103, No.3 (September 1992): 1075-1095.

Erasmus, Udo. *Fats That Heal, Fats That Kill*. Burnaby BC: Alive Books, 1994.

Farlow, Christine Hoza. *Food Additives: A Shopper's Guide to What's Safe & What's Not*. Self Published, 1999.

Frahm, David. *Healthy Habits: 20 Simple Ways to Improve Your Health*. Pinon Press, 1993.

Gates, Donna. *The Body Ecology*. CITY: B.E.D Publications, 1996.

Gittleman, Ann Louise. *Eat Fat, Lose Weight: The Right Fats Can Make You Thin*. Lincolnwood: Keats Publishing, 1999.

Gough, Russell. "The Answer for Toddlers isn't Drugs, it's Patience." *Chronicle Telegram Newspaper*

Health Alert: Mediterranean Diet, Volume 16, Issue 8; Vitamins: The Most Processed Food, Volume 10, Issue 11; Elimination Diet, Volume 11, Issue 4; Low Fat Craze: Volume 12, Issue 4; Violence and Vitamin B, Volume 11, Issue 2.

Landers, Peter. "Study Finds Why Users of Cocaine Get Sick So Often," *The Wallstreet Journal*, (March 6, 2003).

Lyden, Judy. "Don't Take a Teacher's Word That Your Child is Hyperactive." *Chronicle Telegram Newspaper*

Mair, Nancy, Rinzler, Susan, Eds. *Simply Vegetarian: Easy-To-Prepare Recipes For the Vegetarian Gourmet*. Nevada City: DAWN Publications, 1985.

Murray, Michael T. *Understanding Fats & Oils, Your Guide to Healing with Essential Fatty Acids*. Encinitas: Progressive Health Publishing, 1996.

Nelson, Dennis. *Maximizing Your Nutrition*. Self Published, 1988.

Nostrand, Carol A. *Junk Food to Real Food: A Blueprint for Healthier Eating*. New Canaan: Keats Publishing, 1994.

Oski, Frank A. *Don't Drink Your Milk*. Syracuse: Mollica Press, Ltd., 1983.

Ripley, Amanda. "Ritalin: Mom's Little Helper." Time.Com 27 Feb.2001: World Wide Web.

Robertson, Robin. *366 Simply Delicious Dairy-Free Recipes*. New York: Penguin Books, 1997.

Sampson, Hugh A., M.D. "Food Allergy and the Role of Immunotherapy," *The Journal of Allergy and Clinical Immunology*, Vol. 90, No. 2 (August 1992):151-152.

Schlosser, Eric. *Fast Food Nation*. Boston: Houghton Mifflin Company, 2001.

Schmitt, Walter H. *Compiled Notes on Clinical Nutritional Products*. Chapel Hill: David Barmore Productions, YEAR.

"School Lunches Still Inadequate," *The Chronicle Telegram Newspaper*, (May 10, 2003).

School Lunch Program provided by the U.S. Department of Agriculture (USDA)

Siguel, Edward N. *Essential Fatty Acids in Health and Disease*. Brookline: Nutrek Press, 1994.

Spinrad, Leonard. *On This Day in History*. Paramus: Prentice Hall, 1999.

Tressler, Gordon S. *Healthy Habits*. Raleigh: Be Well Publications, 1996.

Thomas, Karen. "Stealing, Dealing and Ritalin." *USA Today* 27 Nov. 2000: D1-2.

Wild Oats Markets, Inc., Independent Publications, 1998.

INDEX

M

Maltose 108

Mannitol 105

Maple Syrup 108

Medication
going off of 141

Mediterranean diet 71

Mediterranean Food Pyramid
186

Mighty meals
Broccoli-Cheese Frittata
164
corn bread 169
dairyless Alfredo Sauce
168
enchilada bake 165
herbed veggie gravy 168
Italian swiss steak 166
macaroni and cheese 166
marvelous meatloaf 167
vegetable chowder 169
zesty cornmeal muffins
170

Molasses 109

Monounsaturated fat 71

N

Naturopaths 127

Nervous System 13

Nutrition facts 65

O

Olive oil 72

Omega 3 31, 42, 71

Omega 6 31, 42

Organic vitamins 117

Organs
system 10

Osteopaths 127

Osteoporosis 89

Oxidation of fats
and cancer 70

P

Pancreas 12
and enzymes 12
insulin 12

Parasites 49
how to get rid of 51
pin worm, common signs
of 50
saliva test 51

Patient's guide 146

Pilot program 149 - 150
feedback after first month
154
feedback after second
month 156
feedback after third month
158
participant history 152
positive experiences from
160

W

Z

"Food is chemistry. Chemistry impacts brain function. Brain function impacts behavior. Thank you, Dr. DeMaria for your part in addressing the connection between diet and behavior. I am a fan!"

Dave Frahm, N.D.
Author, *A Cancer Batttle Plan Sourcebook*
President, HealthQuarters Ministries

Dr. Robert DeMaria's
Training – Teaching – Treating

Dr. DeMaria is available for organizations and individuals for continuing education, seminars, workshops, radio, television interviews and health care evaluations. If you have an organization that needs continuing education credits, Dr. DeMaria can be your next speaker. He has taught for the legal, health, corporate and education professions in the United States and Europe. His enthusiasm is contagious! He has been awarded for his excellence in speaking, writing and leadership skills achieving all world status by several organizations.

Dr. DeMaria treats patients from around the world. Arrangements can be made to receive care for yourself or loved one for chronic and difficult cases. E-mail Dr. DeMaria at DruglessCare@aol.com or call 800-589-4121. Visit his website at www.DrBob4Health.com and sign up for his free weekly health tip.

"Dr. DeMaria presented very useful information helping me to understand living without hormone replacement therapy."

~ Sue Jordan, RN, CFT

"I am glad I went to the seminar. Dr. Bob gave me information that has changed my life."

~ Sue C.

"I wish I would have known more about the Drugless Care that Dr. Bob explains — it was a great seminar!"

~ Gretchen Vendetti, LPN

"The Drugless Approach to HRT was interesting and very informative. Your audience went away with valuable information to 'take charge' of their health."

~ Annette S.

"This class has changed my perception regarding HRT treatment."

~ Cynthia Smallwood, RN, LHN, CHP, MBA

Order Form

Book

☐ *Stop ADHD, ADD, ODD Hyperactivity*
$19.95 each $_____

Audio Programs

Two-Hour Audio Cassette/Disc with Notes:
(Approved by the Ohio Nurse Association)

☐ **Drugless Approach to Hormone**
  Replacement Therapy - Audio $12.95 $_____
                    2 CDs $19.95 $_____

☐ **Drugless Approach to Adrenal**
  & Liver Health - 1 Audio $12.95 $_____
                    2 CDs $19.95 $_____

☐ **For Both Two-Hour Programs -**
                2 Audios $19.95 $_____
                4 CDs $29.95 $_____

For the first book/audio/CD add $5.00 $_____
For each additional book/audio/CD add $3.50 $_____
Ohio residents add 6.75% sales tax $_____

Total $_____

Fax order to 440-322-2502 or
Make checks payable and mail to:
                Drugless Healthcare Solutions
                Dr. Robert DeMaria
                306 Hamilton Circle
                Elyria, OH 44035

Name: _____

Address: _____

_____

City: _____ State: _____ Zip: _____
Telephone: _____
E-mail address: _____

Payment: ☐ Check   ☐ Credit card:
                      ☐ Visa   ☐ MasterCard

Card number: _____ Exp. date: _____

Name on card: _____